High Season
English for the Hotel and Tourist Industry

High Season

English for the Hotel and Tourist Industry

Keith Harding & Paul Henderson

Oxford University Press

OXFORD
UNIVERSITY PRESS

Great Clarendon Street, Oxford OX2 6DP

Oxford University Press is a department of the University of Oxford.
It furthers the University's objective of excellence in research, scholarship,
and education by publishing worldwide in

Oxford New York

Auckland Bangkok Buenos Aires Cape Town Chennai
Dar es Salaam Delhi Hong Kong Istanbul Karachi Kolkata
Kuala Lumpur Madrid Melbourne Mexico City Mumbai
Nairobi São Paulo Shanghai Taipei Tokyo Toronto

OXFORD and OXFORD ENGLISH are registered trade marks of
Oxford University Press in the UK and in certain other countries

ISBN 0 19 451308 4

Typeset in Adobe Garamond and Monotype Gill Sans by Tradespools Ltd,
Frome, Somerset, UK

Printed in China

ACKNOWLEDGEMENTS

The authors would like to thank their families and friends, and their
colleagues and students at St Giles College

*The publishers and authors would also like to thank the following for their kind
permission to use articles, extracts, or adaptations from copyright material:*
Cosmosair plc, Bromley; Thomson Tour Operation Ltd, London; *Hotels and
Restaurants of Britain 1991* and *1993*, Product Communications Ltd; The
Copthorne Tara Hotel, London; 'Tall Story', *Caterer and Hotelkeeper*, 6
February 1992, Reed Business Publishing; Trusthouse Forte plc, London; *The
Business of Hotels*, S. Medlik, Butterworth-Heinemann Ltd 1989; Lodgistix UK
Ltd, Croydon; Forte Crest Hotel, Gloucester; Royal York Hotel, York; *Thomas
Cook Traveller's London 1993* by Kathy Arnold, AA Publishing; 'There's a fly in
my software' © George Cole/The Times Newspapers Ltd, February 1992;
American Express Europe Ltd; Grosvenor House Hotel, London; Abela Hotel,
Monaco; Shearings Ltd, Wigan; *The Business of Tourism*, J. Christopher
Holloway, Pitman Publishing 1989; Evan Evans Tours, London

Every effort has been made to trace the owners of copyright material in
this book, but we should be pleased to hear from any copyright owner
whom we have been unable to contact in order to rectify any errors or
omissions

Illustrations by:
Ken Binder/Satchell Illustrators page 68
Paul Collicutt page 83
Madeleine David page 34
Michael Hill page 96
Mike Ogden pages 54, 121
Oxford Illustrators page 21
Sharon Pallent/Maggie Mundy Illustrators' Agency pages 16, 25, 37
Stuart Robertson/Sharp Practice page 119
Colin Salmon pages 53, 106, 110, 111, 113
Tim Slade pages 38, 110
Darrell Warner page 51
David Williams pages 43, 80

Location Photography by:
Emily Anderson page 127
Philip Dunn pages 31, 36, 42, 50, 57, 64, 70, 74, 77, 79, 100, 133

We would like to thank the following for their permission to
reproduce photographs:
The Abela Hotel, Monaco page 114
Bugsgang and Associates page 138
Colorific! page 20 (Michael Yamashita – health club)
The Copthorne Tara Hotel pages 24, 26 (man in wheelchair x 2)
James Davis pages 10 (manor house), 89 (boat and horseriding), 92
    (houses at dusk), 131
European Tour Operators Association page 109
Life File pages 10 (Eddy Tan – Spanish hotel), 20 (Lionel Moss –
    hotel), 89 (Tim Fisher – museum), 94 (Emma Lee), 135 (Jerry
    Hoare – Lyric Theatre), 136 (Emma Lee)
The Grosvenor House Hotel page 111
Robert Harding page 20 (gym), (Tony Gervis – golf), 91 (Greek
    Dancers), (Peter Ryan – Samarian Gorge), 135 (Windsor Castle)
Archie Miles page 26 (games room)
Product Communications page 28
The Royal York Hotel page 65
Margaret Sesnan page 103
Southern Stock Photo Agency page 92 (Jim Schwabel – all photos of
    Charleston except for houses at dusk)
Tony Stone Worldwide page 10 (holiday villa), 12 (John Warden), 53
    (Vic Thomasson – (women at table), 86 (Robin Smith), 91 (Marcus
    Brooke – Knossos), 97 (Manfred Mehlig – Canterbury), 124 (Alan
    Smith), 135 (Joe Cornish – Houses of Parliament), 137 (Gerrard
    Louce – students, cycling), 139
The Telegraph Colour Library page 22
Thomsons pages 15, 18
Travel Ink Photo Library page 27
The Travel Library page 115 (Philip Enticknap)
TRIP pages 26 (Helene Rogers – courtesy bus), 53 (Helene Rogers –
    gift shop), (Vicky Pimm – face massage), 62 (L. J. Hall), 97 (Roger
    Cracknell – Leeds Castle), 105 (Helene Rogers)

We would also like to thank the following for their help and patience,
and for providing locations, models and photographs:
The Manager and staff of the Feathers Hotel, Woodstock
The Manager and staff of The Holiday Inn, Telford
The Manager and staff of The Holiday Inn, Birmingham
Diane MacLennan of UK Hosts
The Inter-Continental Hotel, London
The Gloucester Hotel, London
The Johnstounburn Hotel, Edinburgh
The King James Thistle Hotel, Edinburgh
The Linden Hotel, Edinburgh
The Copthorne Tara Hotel, London

Typeset in Adobe Garamond and Monotype Gill Sans
by Tradespools Ltd, Frome, Somerset

Contents

		page
1	Types of accommodation	10
2	Hotel facilities	20
3	Staffing and internal organization	31
4	Reservations and check-in	42
5	Hotel and restaurant services	53
6	Money matters	64
7	Dealing with complaints	77
8	Off-site services	89
9	The business traveller	100
10	Conferences	109
11	Tour operation–planning	121
12	Tour operation–execution	133
	Pair/Group A instructions	143
	Pair/Group B instructions	147
	Tapescripts	151
	Wordlist	172

Unit Contents Chart

	Topic	Listening	Speaking	Reading
1	**Types of accommodation** p. 10	Guests' preferences Information about Yosemite	Dealing with enquiries about accommodation	Where to stay in Yosemite Park Brochure descriptions
2	**Hotel facilities** p. 20	At the Hoteliers' Conference Room descriptions	Describing rooms	A room at the Copthorne Tara 'Tall Story'
3	**Staffing and internal organization** p. 31	Hotel staff hierarchy The job of a concierge	Running a small hotel	A family hotel in the Dordogne A job application
4	**Reservations and check-in** p. 42	Telephone reservations Check-in procedure	Reservations procedure Checking in	Reservations and Front Office computer systems A fax reservation
5	**Hotel and restaurant services** p. 53	Ordering a meal Calling Reception	In the restaurant	Menus Hotel notices and information sheets
6	**Money matters** p. 64	Three financial transactions Changes in rates	Checking out	A bill from the Royal York Hotel A memo to staff

Writing	Language study	Word study	Activities
Describing a hotel for a brochure	Giving opinions Expressing likes and dislikes	Accommodation Hotel features	Choosing a hotel Describing beach resort hotels
An informal letter recommending hotels	Describing past time Making comparisons	Guidebook symbols Special facilities	Comparing hotels Prioritizing alteration work on a hotel
A letter of application	Obligation	Adjectives and nouns describing personality	Appointing a concierge Careers in housekeeping and maintenance
Confirming a reservation by fax	Pronunciation of letters Short answers Tag questions	Hotel documents	Allocating rooms Buying a computer system
Taking telephone messages	Intentions and spontaneous decisions Making requests	American and British English	Categorizing jobs in the food and beverage cycle Separating jumbled orders
A letter offering a special rate	Using numbers The Passive	Financial terms	Exchanging foreign currency A comparison of tipping in three countries

	Topic	Listening	Speaking	Reading
7	**Dealing with complaints** p. 77	A guest complains A disastrous experience	People who complain Dealing with complaints	'There's a fly in my software Letters of complaint
8	**Off-site services** p. 89	Excursions on Crete A guided tour of Charleston	Local attractions in Charleston Hiring a car	Off-site services Car hire information
9	**The business traveller** p. 100	Looking after important guests An interview with a businesswoman	Cultural differences	Hotel business facilities The Japanese business traveller
10	**Conferences** p. 109	Inspecting a conference suite Changing a conference programme	Conference facilities	A letter of enquiry from a conference co-ordinator The Abela Hotel, Monaco
11	**Tour operation : planning** p. 121	Explaining 'fam trips' Choosing a hotel for an incentive tour	Arranging an itinerary	Five tour operators Shearings fam trip itinerary
12	**Tour operation : execution** p. 133	Checking in a group Changes in rates	Assessing tour group needs	A Welcome Letter and itinerary A rooming list

Writing	Language study	Word study	Activities
Replying to a letter of complaint	Present Perfect Passive should have (done) Responding to complaints	Intensifying adverbs	Restaurant role play Assessing guests' feedback
Describing local attractions	First Conditional Giving advice	Entertainments, coach tours	Exchanging information about a coach tour Planning a guided tour
A Welcome Letter	Present Perfect Continuous vs Present Perfect Simple	Comparison and contrast	Designing a business apartment Where business travellers stay – an international comparison
A leaflet for a conference hotel	Describing use Talking about room layouts Describing size and dimension	Conferences and meetings	Planning a conference programme Opening night role play
A letter to a tour operator	Future Continuous Future Perfect Reported speech	Prepositional phrases	Hotel manager/tour operator role play Completing a tour-planning diary
A letter in response to survey results	Second Conditional Reported questions	Formal notices	Selecting a resort representative Assessing feedback on package tours

1   Types of accommodation

1 Listening

1   Study the list below, then listen to four hotel users talking about what they think is important in a hotel. Tick (✓) the area(s) that they mention.

	guests			
	1	2	3	4
large rooms				
small hotels				
good facilities				
friendly staff				
near the town centre				
efficient service				

2   The comments you heard were made by the people described below.
Listen to the cassette again and try to match the comments to the people
who made them.

    a ☐ A successful French research scientist who is often invited to speak
at international conferences.

    b ☐ A retired banker from the USA.

    c ☐ The Sales Director of an export company in Turkey.

    d ☐ A travel writer for several British newspapers and magazines who
also presents a television programme on holidays and travel.

2 Language study   Giving opinions

Look at the ways in which the people interviewed gave their opinions:

▶ ***I think** most of the big hotels are so impersonal.*

▶ ***For me**, the ideal hotel has big rooms with comfortable beds . . .*

▶ ***If you ask me**, a hotel that doesn't make you feel really special . . .*

▶ *It **should** also be as near the centre of town as possible . . .*

Can you think of other ways in which people give their opinions?
Now make similar sentences to express your opinion on:

a the hotel industry in your country.

b the President of the USA.

c airline cuisine.

d classical music.

e computers.

f people who drive under the influence of alcohol.

Expressing likes and dislikes

Look at these ways of talking about likes and dislikes. Can you put them
in order from 'like most' (1) to 'dislike most' (10)?

☐ I like smaller hotels.

☐ I love going on vacation, especially in Europe.

☐ I don't mind paying for it.

☐ I enjoy staying in hotels.

☐ I hate flying.

☐ I'm not too keen on Italian cooking.

☐ I can't stand lying on a beach all day.

☐ I hate people who don't say thank you.

☐ We're both fond of walking.

☐ I dislike it when you do that.

Now make similar sentences to say how much you like or dislike the
following:

a Chinese food	**c** sunbathing	**e** driving
b going to the theatre	**d** visiting art galleries	**f** rain

3 Word study

Working in pairs, divide the following words into groups. Then compare your groups with those of another pair.

coffee shop	elegant	simple	cabin	rate	splendid
reservation	stables	rustic	luxurious	parking	lounge
golf-course	fireplace	trail	suite	sturdy	price
comfortable	attractive	fee	tent	elaborate	campsite

4 Reading

Read the passage opposite, taken from an American guidebook describing accommodation in Yosemite National Park in California. Complete the grid below.

Accommodation	Size	Room types	Price	Facilities	Other info.
Ahwahnee Hotel	*123 rooms and 5 suites*	*single room/ cottage* *double room/ cottage* *suite*	*$196* *$202* *from $375*		
Yosemite Lodge				*shops, lounge, 2 restaurants, coffee shop, cafeteria*	
Wawona Hotel					*4 miles inside south gateway*
Camping					

Where to stay

From luxury hotel to simple tent, Yosemite offers a wide choice of accommodations. Reservations are advised at all times, and especially in summer. For stays during the summer season and holidays, make reservations as far as one year in advance to avoid being disappointed. Write to the Yosemite Park & Curry Co., Reservation Department, 5410 E. Home Ave., Fresno, CA 93727 (tel. 209/252-4848).

The Ahwahnee Hotel
Yosemite Village. Tel 209/252-4848. 123 rms. 5 suites.

$ Rates: $196 single room or cottage. $202 double room or cottage, from $375 suite. Lower midweek winter rates are available.

Luxurious and very centrally located, the Ahwahnee is the park's premiere hostelry. A short, signposted walk from Yosemite Village, this lovely hotel was built in 1927 from local rock. Rooms are both comfortable and elegant, with full baths, and sturdy, rustic wooden furniture. Suites include an additional sitting-room. The hotel's celebrated dining and entertainment facilities include the Indian Bar Room for drinks and the splendid Dining Room, where dinner reservations are required year round.

Yosemite Lodge
near the foot of Yosemite Falls. Tel. 209/252-4848. 600 rms and cabins (150 with bath).

$ Rates: $43 single or double without bath, $40 cabin without bath; $75 single or double with bath, $52 cabin with bath.

Yosemite Lodge is within easy walking distance of most of the valley's attractions. It offers attractive but simple hotel rooms and small redwood cabins. Because it's priced so well, this place is popular, and reservations should be made as far in advance as possible. Facilities include a coffee shop, lounge, two restaurants, and a cafeteria, as well as several shops.

Wawona Hotel
4 miles inside the south gateway. Tel. 209/252-4848. 104 rms.

$ Rates: $55 single or double without bath, $74 single or double with bath.

You won't be roughing it at the Wawona, near the southern end of Yosemite. This is the oldest hotel in continuous service in the national park system, dating from 1879. The pretty wooden structures offer comfortable, if sparsely furnished, rooms; facilities include a swimming-pool, a tennis court, and a nine-hole golf-course, as well as nearby stables.

Camping

Yosemite's 300-plus year-round campsites expand to a whopping 2,000 sites in summer. Campground fees range from $4 to $12 per day. Sites are scattered over 20 different campgrounds, and split into two categories. The $7 to $12 Type A sites are the most elaborate, with well-defined roads, parking, drinking water, flush toilets, and, generally, a fireplace, table/bench combination, and tent space. The $4 Type B sites may be accessible by road or trail, and conveniences are limited to basic sanitary facilities and a smattering of fireplaces and tables.

From June 1 to September 15 camping permits are limited to 7 days in the valley and 14 days in the rest of the park. The rest of the year campers can stay for as long as 30 days.

For more details on campgrounds, contact the Campground Office, P.O. Box 577, Yosemite National Park, CA 95389 tel. 209/372-0265 or 372-0200.

Source: Frommer's California

Vocabulary
roughing it = living without the usual comforts of life
whopping = huge, very big
a smattering of = a few

5 Listening   **1**   Listen to these two telephone calls to the California Travel Bureau in London. Complete the information in the chart which follows. Leave blank the column headed 'You'.

Name	Ms Wallace	Mr Curtis	You
Date of visit to Yosemite			
Number of people			
Accommodation requirements			
Address			

2   Look at the following expressions, most of which are used in the dialogues. Three of them are *not* used. Listen again to the cassette and identify the three expressions which are not used.

a Can I help you?
b Could you give me some information about accommodation?
c I wonder if you could help me?
d Could you give me your name and address?
e I'm trying to find out about accommodation.
f Is there anything else?
g Certainly.
h How may I help you?
i What would you like to know?
j I'd like some information, please.
k Could you possibly send me details?
l Would you like me to send you some information?

6 Speaking   Work in pairs. Each partner should fill in the column in the table headed 'You', then act out similar conversations. Take it in turns to play the part of the customer.

7 Reading   **1**   Look at the following brochure descriptions of the Hotel Arina Sands. What information can you find about:

a size and location?
b comfort and atmosphere?
c entertainment for family and children?
d entertainment and local facilities?

Hotel Arina Sands
★ ★ ★ ★
Kokkini Hani

'With its fine beach facilities and splendid organized entertainments, the Arina Sands is an ideal choice for families with children.'

Official Rating: A category

This lively self-contained hotel development stands right beside a long sandy beach just a few minutes walk from the resort centre. Brightly furnished in a traditional Cretan style, its comfortable rooms are located both in the main hotel and in adjoining bungalows. Staff are friendly and helpful and top family attractions include its well run children's amenities and marvellous entertainment programmes. Local sports and shopping facilities are also good and you'll find plenty of nearby bars and tavernas. From here buses run regularly along the coast to the capital Heraklion.

- *Large pool*
- *Poolside bar*
- *Main bar*
- *Air-conditioned throughout*
- *2 lounges including one with TV area*
- *Buffet-style restaurant with pool views*
- *Traditional taverna*
- *Shops*
- *Basketball, volleyball*
- *Tennis and squash*
- *Aerobics*
- *Watersports from beach*
- *Table tennis, darts, pool table*
- *Full entertainment programme including shows and cabarets*
- *Weekly Cretan evening*
- *Disco*
- *Children's pool, organized games and events, mini-club, playroom, playground, highchairs, early suppers and babysitting on request*
- *Lifts*

Hotel Arina Sands

Kokkini Hani   ★ ★ ★ ★

OUR OPINION *A spacious hotel with good facilities and a gorgeous beach. Ideal for families.*

The Arina Sands is a large and comfortable hotel, especially popular with families, that's situated right above a superb, sandy beach. Friendly and informal, with a reputation for typical Greek hospitality and good food, it has organized fun and games for children in our Big T Club; while mums and dads will enjoy the chance to unwind and soak up the sun.

- ☼ pool; sun terrace; gardens
- ☼ bar/lounge; poolside taverna
- ☼ all meals buffet service
- ☼ tennis; table tennis; organized games and competitions
- ☼ TV room; games room
- ☼ Greek/Cretan evenings with live music and folk dancing (high season, weather permitting); occasional barbecues; nightclub and disco with shows
- ☼ shops
- ☼ children's playground; playroom; early suppers;
- ☼ highchairs available

Source: Cosmosair plc   *Source: Thomson Tour Operator Ltd*

2 Which description makes the hotel sound more appealing? Why?

8 Word study   **1**   Which adjectives can be used with which nouns? Tick (✓) the
appropriate boxes:

	room	view	staff	entertainment
spacious	☐	☐	☐	☐
gorgeous	☐	☐	☐	☐
superb	☐	☐	☐	☐
comfortable	☐	☐	☐	☐
marvellous	☐	☐	☐	☐
friendly	☐	☐	☐	☐
lively	☐	☐	☐	☐

2   Match the sentences to the numbers in the picture.

a It's got arched windows.
b There's an oval swimming-pool.
c There are sun-loungers by the pool.
d The building is three storeys high.
e It's got a sloping roof.
f The roof is flat.

Can you think of some more adjectives which describe shape and an appropriate noun connected with hotels for each one? Add them to these lists.

Adjectives	Nouns
oval	swimming-pool
arched	window
sloping	roof

9 Activity

What do you think the following people would require from a hotel?

a Intercontinental airline staff on a break between flights.
b A couple on their honeymoon.
c A group of four student friends travelling in their summer vacation.

Make notes in pairs under the headings below, then compare your notes with those of another pair. Discuss any differences.

location	comfort	value
a		
b		
c		

facilities	service	entertainment
a		
b		
c		

10 Activity

Divide into pairs, **A** and **B**.

A

You are a tour operator. You have a series of pictures of beach resort hotels which you want to include in your summer brochure (see below). However, you do not have the names of the hotels with the pictures. You have phoned a representative of the hotel chain (B) who has the information you need. Describe the pictures you have and find out the names. Ask questions to check.

Question prompts:
Has it got . . . ?
How many . . . ?
Is there a . . . ?/Are there any . . . ?
What shape is . . . ?

B

Your instructions are on page 147.

11 Writing   Use the Arina Sands brochure descriptions in *7 Reading* as models to write a similar brochure entry for one of the hotels pictured in *10 Activity*. Show your description to a partner and see if they can recognize which of the hotels it is.

12 Vocabulary

accessible p. 13, that can be reached

adjoining p. 15, next to each other

air-conditioned p. 15, with temperature and humidity controlled

amenities p. 15, places to go and things to do

bonus p. 151 (tapescript), something pleasant in addition to what was expected

brochure p. 18, booklet containing information about something

budget p. 29, amount of money available for a specific purpose

buffet service p. 15, where guests serve themselves from a number of dishes

bungalows p. 15, small houses with one storey

business centre p. 151 (tapescript), room(s) with office facilities available to guests at a hotel

cabin p. 12, small hut made of wood

celebrated p. 13, famous

chain p. 18, group of hotels owned by the same person or company

conveniences p. 13, facilities

de luxe p. 151 (tapescript), luxurious

designated areas p. 151 (tapescript), areas marked out for a particular purpose

elaborate p. 12, carefully made and highly developed

expand p. 13, grow

facilities p. 10, equipment

fee p. 12, charge

folk dancing p. 15, traditional dancing of a community or country

high season p. 15, the part of the year with the most guests

honeymoon p. 17, holiday taken by a newly married couple

hospitality p. 15, friendly and generous treatment of guests

in advance p. 13, beforehand; ahead in time

live music p. 15, music that is performed (i.e. not recorded)

lodge p. 13, country house or cabin

luxurious p. 12, very comfortable

permits p. 13, official documents that give sb the right to go somewhere or do sth

range from ... to p. 13, vary between specified limits

resort p. 15, holiday town

rustic p. 12, typical of the country or country people

sanitary facilities p. 13, toilets, washrooms, etc.

self-contained p. 15, with no shared facilities

spacious p. 16, with a lot of space

sparsely furnished p. 13, with little furniture

split into p. 13, divided into

stables p. 12, buildings in which horses are kept

sturdy p. 12, strong and solid

suite p. 12, hotel bedroom with an adjoining living-room

throughout p. 15, everywhere

trail p. 12, path through the country

unwind p. 15, relax, especially after hard work

within (easy) reach p. 151 (tapescript), at a distance that can be (easily) travelled

2 Hotel facilities

1 Word study

Match the hotel guidebook symbols opposite with the facilities listed below. A few have been done for you.

- ☐ tennis
- ☐ telephone in bedrooms
- ☐ parking
- ☐ conferences
- ☐ central heating
- ☐ TV in bedrooms
- ☐ foreign language spoken
- ☐ facilities for disabled
- ☐ morning coffee/snacks
- ☐ bar
- ☐ mini-bar in bedrooms
- ☐ swimming-pool
- ☐ fishing

- ☐ special Christmas arrangements
- ☐ recreation/games room
- ☐ laundry/valet service
- ☐ four-poster bed
- ☐ building of historic interest
- ☐ children welcomed
- ☐ solarium
- ☐ night porter
- ☐ dogs allowed
- ☐ golf-course (9 holes)
- ☐ golf-course (18 holes)
- ☐ air-conditioning

Key to Symbols

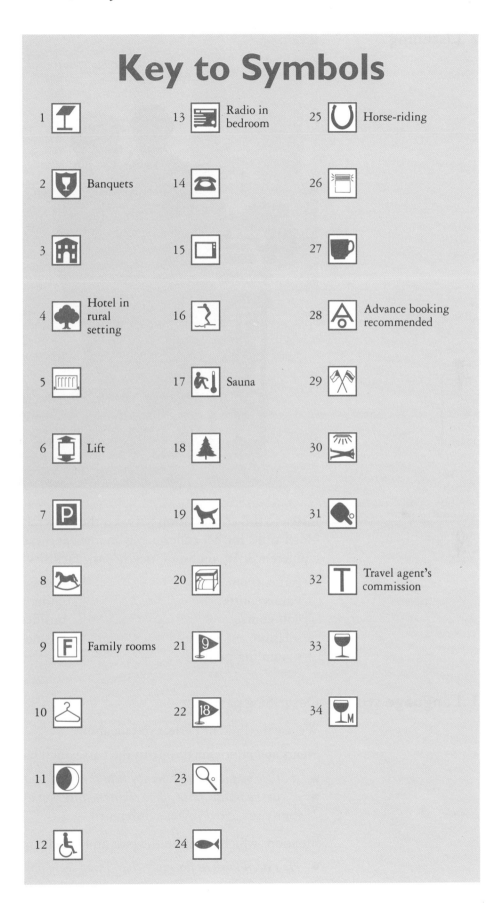

1

13 Radio in bedroom

25 Horse-riding

2 Banquets

14

26

3

15

27

4 Hotel in rural setting

16

28 Advance booking recommended

5

17 Sauna

29

6 Lift

18

30

7

19

31

8

20

32 Travel agent's commission

9 Family rooms

21

33

10

22

34

11

23

12

24

2   Listening

Listen to this conversation between the General Manager of the Palace Hotel and a former colleague, who meet at the annual Hoteliers' Conference. As you listen, tick (✔) the facilities that the hotel has *now*.

☐ games room   ☐ fitness centre
☐ tennis courts   ☐ sauna
☐ golf-course   ☐ business apartments
☐ solarium   ☐ business centre
☐ swimming-pool   ☐ conference rooms

3   Language study

Describing past time

We use the Present Perfect to talk about:

events at an undefined time in the past which have a result in the present.

▶ ... *they've put a lot of money into the hotel, and it really looks great now.*
▶ ... *we've made quite a few changes since you were there.* (You were there four years ago. Now it's different.)

situations which began in the past and which are still continuing.

▶ *He's been with us for more than three years now ...*

We use the Simple Past to describe events at a particular time in the past.

▶ *We **built** a large extension a couple of years ago . . .*
▶ *Last year we **converted** them into business apartments and a business centre.*
▶ *He **left** just after you, I think.*
▶ *. . . in the end, we **hired** a top French chef.*

Now write out the following sentences in full, using the Present Perfect or the Simple Past:

a 'When (they/arrive)?' 'Two weeks ago.'
b In January, we (employ) three new members of staff.
c I (not/see) Samantha since February.
d The guests (be) tired after their long journey.
e Last year, prices (go up) by five per cent.
f Our current chef (work) here for over a year.
g We (decide) to buy it as soon as we saw it.
h As you can see, we (finish) building the extension.

Making comparisons

Look at how we compare things:

▶ *Yes, things are **better than** they were four years ago, that's for sure . . .*
▶ *Our rooms are **far more comfortable** . . .*
▶ *. . . we offer **the best** facilities in the area.*

Now study this extract from a consumer guide which compares single rooms in competing Italian hotels. Make sentences comparing them.

	Hotel Albani	Hotel Concordia	Hotel Moderno
Price	■ ■	■ ■ ■	■
Size	■	■ ■ ■	■ ■
Comfort	■ ■ ■	■ ■	■
Facilities	■ ■	■ ■ ■	■
Distance from city centre	■	■ ■	■ ■ ■

4 Reading

1 Read this description of a 'Classic Room' at the Copthorne Tara Hotel in London and make a list of all the facilities and furniture in the room.

Far from being places used only for sleeping — and yes, the beds are exceptionally comfortable — our *Classic Rooms* make waking hours fly. With their subtle colours and lime-oak furnishings, they're light, spacious, and charming; ideal for working (there's a large, business-like desk) or relaxing (there's satellite TV with three international channels; a radio, a computerized mini-bar; facilities for making your own tea and coffee; two extremely restful armchairs ...).

A bedside panel gives remote control of lighting, TV, radio, and signs for 'Make Up Room' and 'Do Not Disturb'.

A trouser-press, iron, and board keep creases razor sharp or invisible as required. An air-and-temperature control system ensures an atmosphere perfect for individual requirements.

This level of thoughtful comfort extends into beautifully designed bathrooms with basins, showers, and baths.

And if visitors want anything else, they can always dial room service *24 hours a day.*

2 What adjectives are used to describe:
  a the room as a whole?
  b the bed?
  c the desk?
  d the armchairs?
  e the bathroom?

Make a list of alternative adjectives that could be used to describe each of these.

5 Listening

1 Listen to these phone calls between a prospective guest and the information desk at three different hotels. The guest is enquiring about the different rooms available. As you listen, identify which of the following rooms are being described.

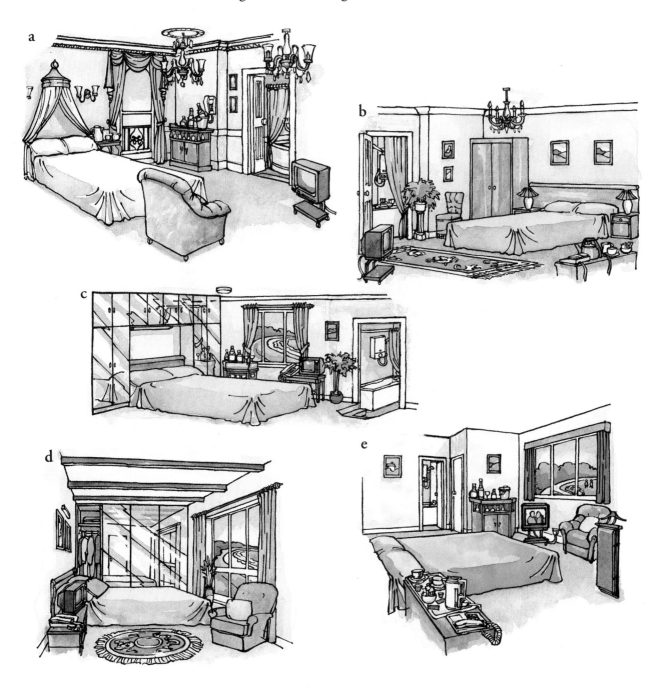

2 Listen again and say how you feel each receptionist behaves. Are they:

a interested/persuasive?
b bored?

How do you know?

6 Speaking

Prepare a description in note form of one of the two remaining rooms described in *5 Listening*. Your partner should prepare the other. Practise giving the information in pairs. First, one of you is the receptionist and the other a caller. The receptionist must try to be persuasive and interested. Then change roles.

7 Word study

Many guests have special needs. What extra facilities would the following people require or find useful? Match with the column on the right.

1 a person in a wheelchair	a organized games and activities
2 an elderly person	b nappy-changing facilities in toilets
3 a family with a baby	c a resident nurse
4 a family with young children	d push-chairs
5 a blind person	e special wide doors
	f a courtesy bus to the town centre
	g ramps at all stairs
	h a playground and/or play-room
	i hoists in bedrooms
	j lifts to all floors
	k notices in Braille
	l a low-level front desk

8 Reading

1 The text which follows includes measurements in feet and inches, which are still used to talk about people's height in some English-speaking countries. However, it is easy to calculate the equivalent height in metres.

1 foot (') = 30 cm   1 inch (") = 2.5 cm

5 feet   = 5 × 30 cm = 1.5 m   6 inches = 6 × 2.5 cm = 15 cm

So five feet six (5' 6") = 1.5 m + 15 cm, which is 1.65 m.

2 What problems do tall people face in hotels? Make a list, then read the text below to check if your ideas are included. What other problems are mentioned in the text?

Tall Story

While small may be beautiful, tall is just plain uncomfortable it seems, particularly when it comes to staying in hotels and eating in restaurants.

The Tall Persons Club Great Britain, which was formed six months ago to campaign for the needs of the tall, has turned its attention to hotels and restaurants.

Beds that are too small, shower heads that are too low, and restaurant tables with scarcely any leg-room all make life difficult for those of above average height, it claims.

But it is not just the extra-tall whose needs are not being met. The average height of the population has been increasing steadily yet the standard size of beds, doorways, and chairs has remained unchanged.

"The bedding industry says a bed should be six inches larger than the person using it, so even a king size bed at 6'6" is falling short for 25% of men, while the standard 6'3" bed caters for less than half of the male population," said 6'8" club president Phil Heinricy.

Besides 7' long beds, Mr Heinricy wants to see shower heads with longer adjusting rails and a taller easy chair in hotel rooms. If not supplied as standard, then he believes at least 5% of rooms should

cater for the taller person, who would be prepared to pay more.

Similarly restaurant tables can cause no end of problems. Small tables, which mean the long-legged have to sit a foot or so away from them, are enough to make tall clients go elsewhere.

Some have already taken note, however. At Queens Moat Houses' Caledonian Hotel in Edinburgh, 6'6" beds are now installed as standard after requests for longer beds from taller visitors, particularly Americans.

One supplier to have recognized the increasing size of its clients is Corby Trouser Presses, which has added two inches to the height of its presses.

3 **a** What other words or expressions are used to describe tall people?
   b Who exactly is affected by this problem?
   c What solutions are being suggested?
   d What steps have already been taken?

9 Activity

Below are the entries for three hotels in Edinburgh from a guidebook about where to stay in the United Kingdom.

1 a Which hotel is not in the centre of Edinburgh?
  b Which hotel is the largest?
  c Which is the smallest?
  d Which hotel has Oriental cuisine?
  e Which hotel does not include breakfast in its basic room rate?
  f What facilities are common to all three hotels?

1

**Edinburgh Lothian
Johnstounburn House Hotel**

**Humbie EH36 5PL
Tel: Humbie (0875) 833696 Fax: (0875) 833626
Manager: Ken Chernoff
Mount Charlotte Thistle Hotels**

17th century country house hotel set in acres of lawns, gardens, and farm land, at the foot of the beautiful Lammermuir Hills, fifteen miles from Edinburgh. 20 bedrooms of distinction with private bathrooms. Scottish Tourist Board Commended.

Map Ref: 32C3
STB 4 Crown Commended, AA ***, RAC ***
FULLY LICENSED
Open all the year
Single bedroom fr £90.00 per day
Double bedroom fr £125.00 per day
Full breakfast included
Full breakfast £7.50
Lunch fr £12.00/alc Dinner fr £26.00/alc
Restaurant: Contemporary Scottish
Open: Lunch, 12-2pm Dinner 7-9pm
Seats: 40

2

**Edinburgh Lothian
King James Thistle Hotel**

**St James Centre, EH1 3SW
Tel: Edinburgh (031) 556 0111 Telex: 727200
Mount Charlotte Thistle Hotels**

Just off world-famous Princes Street, the hotel is a great place to return to after a day spent exploring the Castle, the Royal Mile, and the city's celebrated galleries and gardens or after a tiring day's business. 147 rooms, all with bathroom. French Brasserie and American themed bar.

Map ref: 32B3
THISTLE ****
FULLY LICENSED
Open all the year
Single bedroom with bath fr £72.00 per day
Double bedroom with bath fr £90.00 per day
Full Breakfast £8.25 Continental £6.25
Lunch fr £7.50/alc Dinner fr £11.50/alc
Restaurant: French cuisine
Open: Lunch 12.30-2pm Dinner 6.30-10pm
Weekend rates available

3

**Edinburgh Lothian Linden
Hotel and Buntoms
Thai Restaurant**

**9/13 Nelson Street, EH3 6LF
Tel: (031) 557 4344
Proprietor: Mr Buntom Dejrudee
Manager: Mr Anthony Carrigan**

Central Edinburgh hotel in fine Georgian terrace close to town centre with Scotland's first Thai restaurant. 20 bedrooms (with and without facilities) in well-established small hotel providing good value for money. Bar. Night porter. Close to theatres and shops.

Map ref: 32B3
Edinburgh Tourist Board
FULLY LICENSED
Open all the year
Single bedroom fr £32.00 per day
with bath/shower fr £39.00 per day
Double bedroom fr £44.00 per day
with bath/shower fr £55.00 per day
Full breakfast included
Lunch fr £7.00 Tea fr £2.50
Dinner fr £10.00. Thai cuisine. Seats 70
10% service charge added in restaurant

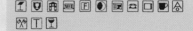

2 a Which hotel would you like to stay in? Why?
  b Are any of the hotels suitable for the guests profiled at the start of Unit 1? Match them up if possible.

10 Activity   The White Lion Hotel is old. Hotel inspectors have just visited it and made a number of recommendations for structural changes and new facilities to fit in with government regulations and allow guests with special needs to stay.

1   Read the list of recommendations.
    a   Which do you think are essential?
    b   Establish an order of priority.

Recommendation	Priority	Approx. cost
Install lift to upper floors	☐	£8,000
Widen doors to all communal rooms	☐	£1,000
Build safety-rail on steps to entrance	☐	£500
Build outside fire-escape (from upper floors)	☐	£2,000
Build extra toilets (including one with wheelchair access) near bar, to replace existing outside toilets	☐	£2,000
Fit smoke alarms	☐	£200
Install electric stair-lift for wheelchair access to first floor (alternative to existing hidden service lift)	☐	£1,000
Put ramps on all outside steps	☐	£500

2   The hotel owners have calculated how much each alteration will probably cost. In addition to the inspectors' recommendations, they also want to make other changes to improve the hotel. They have a total budget of £30,000 for all the alterations.

In groups, look at the two lists and decide what you are going to spend the money on. Then compare with another group.

Alteration	Approx. cost
Redecorate throughout hotel	£3,000
Install central heating on top floor (other floors already have it)	£2,000
Convert attic to extra room	£4,000
Build extension on bar (extra seating)	£9,000
Build children's play area in corner of garden	£2,500
Build tennis courts in grounds	£3,000
Refit all bathrooms (twenty rooms)	£1,000 per room

11 Writing   Choose any two of the three hotels from *9 Activity* and write a letter recommending them to a friend who is planning to visit Edinburgh.

12 Vocabulary

adjusting p. 27, that can be changed

annexe p. 152 (tapescript), extra building added to a larger one

attic p. 29, room at the top of a building in the roof

communal rooms p. 29, rooms for everyone to use

conferences p. 20, formal meetings for discussion or exchange of views between people who have the same interests or are in the same business, **conference (rooms)** p. 22

converted into p. 23, changed into

courtesy bus p. 26, bus service provided by a hotel free of charge

disabled p. 20, people who are unable to use all of the parts of their body

en suite p. 153 (tapescript), with a bath and/or shower attached

exceptionally p. 24, extremely

extension p. 23, part of a building that has been added later

fire escape p. 29, way (usually stairs) by which people can leave a burning building

fitness centre p. 22, special room or rooms for doing exercises and physical training

full-length mirrors p.153 (tapescript), long mirrors in which a person can see their whole body

furnishings p. 24, furniture, equipment, fittings, etc. in a room

hoists p. 26, devices which lift people who are not able to lift themselves

homely p. 153 (tapescript), simple but comfortable

install p. 29, put in place

king-size p. 27, extra large

laundry/valet service p. 20, service for washing and cleaning clothes

nappy-changing facilities p. 26, equipment and place where a baby can be cleaned and changed

occupancy rates p. 152 (tapescript), the number of rooms actually used by guests compared to the total number of rooms available

panoramic p. 153 (tapescript), offering a wide and beautiful view

paying off p. 152 (tapescript), bringing benefits

ramps p. 26, sloping surfaces to let wheeled vehicles go up stairs

recommendation p. 29, strong suggestion to do something

recreation p. 20, relaxation and entertainment

refit p. 29, replace and put in new equipment

remote control p. 24, system of controlling something (e.g. a television) from a distance

room service p. 24, hotel service by which food, drink, etc. are sent up to a guest's room

safety rail p. 29, metal or wooden bar to help or protect people (e.g. to hold on to when climbing up steps)

solarium p. 20, room where a person can lie and be exposed to bright artificial sunlight

stair-lift p. 29, device to move disabled people up stairs

subtle p. 24, designed to have a clever effect, but without being noticed

take-over p. 152 (tapescript), act of buying and taking control of a business by another business

trouser-press p. 24, device for ironing and pressing a pair of trousers

3 Staffing and internal organization

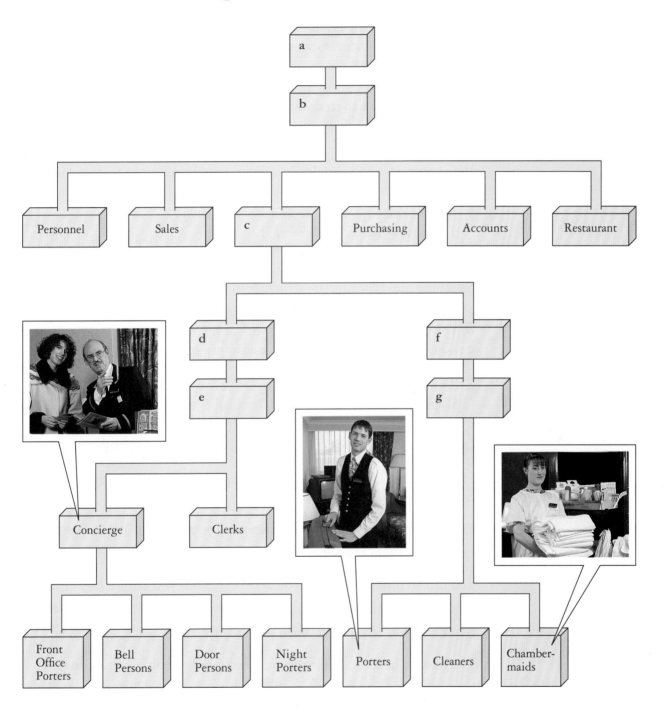

1 Listening

1 Above is a simplified staff tree of a medium-sized hotel. Without writing the words in, can you suggest the names of the missing jobs?

2 Listen and complete the table.

2 Language study   Obligation

We use **must**, **have to**, and **should** to talk about obligation:

▶ *The house manager . . . **must** make sure the hotel stays profitable.*
▶ *I **have to** supervise Front-of-House operations.*
▶ *He **should** ensure close liaison between Front-of-House operations and Housekeeping.*

We use **don't have to** to show something is not necessary:

▶ *He **doesn't have to** check with me about day-to-day issues.*

We use **mustn't** and **shouldn't** to indicate obligation **not** to do something:

▶ *We **mustn't** forget that our aim is to make money.*
▶ *I know I **shouldn't** say this but . . .*

1 The housekeeper is explaining to a new chambermaid what her duties are. Select the most appropriate structure in the sentences below:

a You (mustn't/don't have to) smoke in the bedrooms.
b You (don't have to/shouldn't) work at night.
c You (should/don't have to) have a twenty-minute break every two hours.
d You (don't have to/must) make sure you are ready to start work at 8.15 a.m.
e You (have to/shouldn't) be finished by about 2 p.m. most days.
f You (shouldn't/don't have to) make it clear you want a tip.

2 Here are some facts about Britain. Complete the passage by guessing the missing ages.

You don't have to stay at school after the age of [1]_____. At this age, you can marry or join the armed forces with your parents' consent.

You can go into a pub when you are [2]_____ but you cannot buy or drink alcohol there until you are [3]_____. However, you needn't be so old to buy a pet. You can do this when you are just [4]_____.

You need to be [5]_____ before you are allowed to hold a car driving licence or hold any firearm, but you will not be allowed to serve on a jury or vote in general and local elections until you are [6]_____.

3 Write similar sentences about your country.

3 Word study   **1**   Decode the anagram adjectives to find words used to describe personality, and write them in the table below:

   a Mr Thomas has a reputation for being very **ricesen**. However, people don't always appreciate hearing the truth.

   b If you could be a little more **cultunap** in the future, our meetings could start on time for a change.

   c She's extremely **blareeli**. I wouldn't hesitate to give her more responsibility.

   d A good host should always be **utocusero** and serve his guests first.

   e I'm not terribly **carticlap**, I'm afraid. I can't even fix a plug when it goes wrong.

   f You have to be **lebelfix** in this job because half of the year we work shifts.

   g I'm really **suiteachtins** about my new job. There are great opportunities for me.

   h People who are **usitomabi** will get promotion more easily.

   i To get the work done in time you'll need to be very **nicefitfe**.

   j She is very **nitfecnod** that she'll be able to get the work done in time without any problems.

2   Now write out the noun form for each adjective.

adjective	noun

4 Reading   Small hotels have quite different staffing requirements from large ones.

1   Read the text below and decide which of the following titles is the most
          appropriate: *Thanks a Lot!, A Family Affair,* or *All Work and No Play.*

Gérard and Sylvie Bonnet have been sharing the duties of running their ten-bedroomed hotel in the Dordogne for the past fifteen months. In that time, they have taken just three days off work: two for funerals and one for a wedding (their own). On my travels, I have met quite a few of these young, workaholic hoteliers. 'What makes you do it?' I ask Gérard, whose arms are plunged deep in soapy water.

'We both used to work for a large, famous hotel in Paris,' he replies. 'I became the Front Office Manager and Sylvie was my assistant. It was great, but after a while we felt that we needed a change. We wanted a challenge!' It was not long before Gérard was faced with one which came as an inheritance: 'Le Petit Bijou'. They have not looked back since.

'We have a very regular clientele, which we inherited with the building', adds Sylvie. 'This means it has been easy to plan ahead, but naturally there has been some resistance to change. For example, I was about to fill in the old well at the front of the drive with concrete, but some of the guests made such a lot of fuss that I couldn't!'

'The best thing about running a small hotel', says Gérard in his impeccable English, 'is that we can provide our guests with the personal touch. Only having a few customers at a time, I soon learnt how Monsieur Lefevre likes his eggs cooked and what brand of cigarette he smokes.'

Of course, the smaller hotel suffers from a slower turnover of stock. Unusual items might simply perish of old age while waiting to be used. Sylvie's solution is simple: 'If we suddenly need something, we send out "petit Jacques" to the local hypermarket.' Only nineteen,

Jacques, Gérard's younger brother, also came with the hotel. He exudes Gallic charm and wit and genuinely does not seem to mind the heavy workload.

Set in the stunning green paradise that is the Lot, Le Petit Bijou looks set for a rosy future. Tourists flock to the area in their thousands come summer. But a low occupancy rate in the winter quarter means the Bonnets have fewer permanent staff than they would like. Fortunately, they do not suffer from the high labour turnover rate that some small hotels do, but that is because they rely heavily on the largely untrained help of family and friends when the big rush is on.

From my bedroom window, admiring the view, I see Gérard loading his Citroën van with produce from the kitchen garden at the back of the house. 'In the low season we produce more than we need, so we sell any extra to the local stores. I try to get the best price, but I'm not so good at – how do you say – bargaining?', he tells me over a glass of wine at dinner on the eve of my departure.

Source: Michael Blackburn

2 **a** When did the Bonnets start running their own hotel?

    b How is business going?

    c Why did Sylvie not fill in the well?

3 Read the text more carefully and make a note of the advantages and disadvantages of running a small hotel that Gérard and Sylvie have encountered. Can you think of any not mentioned in the text?

4 Write sentences to explain the following vocabulary from the text.

    a regular clientele

    b personal touch

    c slower turnover of stock

    d Jacques . . . also came with the hotel

    e heavy workload

    f low occupancy rate

    g high labour turnover rate

    h the big rush

    i bargaining

    Example:

    A 'regular clientele' means customers who repeatedly visit an establishment.

5 Speaking

Imagine you and three/four partners have enough money to buy and run a small hotel. Think about the following questions:

    a Which country/city/town/village/street would it be in?

    b How many rooms? With what sort of views?

    c What kind of clientele would you try to attract?

    d What special activities would you offer?

    e What would you call it?

    f How would you divide the work?

    g Which jobs would you like most?

    h Which jobs would you like least?

Make notes to help you report to the rest of the class later.

6 Listening

Listen to Christopher Lloyd, the Personnel Director of a large hotel, describing the job of a concierge.

1 As you listen, tick (✓) the items below if you hear Christopher Lloyd talk about them.

☐ personality required
☐ working hours
☐ duties
☐ uniform

2 Listen again and take more detailed notes about the items you ticked.

3 Without listening again, match the halves of the phrases below:

1	provide for	a	a guest's requests
2	contact	b	a courteous manner
3	make	c	guests' needs
4	display	d	a supply of stamps
5	maintain	e	external companies
6	keep	f	guest satisfaction
7	fulfil	g	bookings for tours, etc.
8	maximize	h	a log-book

7 Reading

Read the job advertisement, then complete the letter of application using the following words:

delegates, House, interested, command, apply, get, suitable, Co-ordinator, advertised, had, available, experience, past, chain

CONFERENCE CO-ORDINATOR

We have an interesting opportunity for an enthusiastic person to handle conference requirements as leader of a friendly team based at our prestigious Boston hotel. Applicants will need to have international conference experience and the ability to liaise at all levels.

Working conditions, salary, and benefits are excellent.

Interested applicants with relevant experience should write with their cv to:

Christine Lloyd, Group Personnel Manager, The International Exchange Hotel, Diamond Road, Boston, MA 02107, USA.

36 rue du Bouloi,
33100 Bordeaux
France

14 September 199__

Christine Lloyd
The International Exchange Hotel
Diamond Road
Boston
MA 02107
USA

Dear Ms Lloyd

I am writing to [1]_____ for the post of Conference Co-ordinator as [2]_____ in this month's edition of 'Caterer and Hotelkeeper' magazine. I am particularly [3]_____ in this job as I wish to work in America in order to improve my English and [4]_____ further [5]_____ of hotel work.

I feel I would be [6]_____ for the job as I have the relevant experience and training. For the [7]_____ two years, I have been working as Assistant [8]_____ for a large international [9]_____ of hotels. Recently, I have [10]_____ to co-ordinate a large-scale international conference with over 400 [11]_____ from thirteen countries. I also have three years' valuable Front-of- [12]_____ Management experience and a French Diploma in Hotel Management.

As well as speaking French, I have a good [13]_____ of English and I speak some Spanish and German. I shall be [14]_____ for interview from the middle of August.

I enclose my résumé.

Yours sincerely

Marie-Victoire Dechet

Marie-Victoire Dechet
Enc.

8 Writing

Read the advertisement below and write a letter applying for the job, inventing the necessary work experience for a strong candidate. Try to use some of the expressions from *7 Reading*.

Ellerton House Hotel, Toronto

290-roomed ★★★★ hotel situated in the heart of Toronto requires:

Assistant Front-of-House Manager

The suitable candidate should have a complete knowledge of computer Front Office systems, be a good team leader possessing training and room management skills, have high standards in customer care, sales awareness, and experience of duty management. Please contact: K. Holcroft, Personnel Director, 53 St. Ermin's Street, Toronto, Canada.

9 Activity

In this activity you must work in pairs to decide who is going to get the position of Concierge (Head Hall Porter) in a busy hotel. One of you is the Front-of-House Manager and the other is the General Manager of the hotel.

First, remind yourselves of the job requirements by looking at your notes from *6 Listening* about the role of the Concierge. Then look at the interview notes on the following page and decide who is the best candidate for the job.

MOUNT ROYAL HOTEL
SAN FRANCISCO

INTERVIEW NOTES

Concierge (Head Hall Porter) July 19th

Name	Sandra Boero
Age	32
Education	Completed High School
Languages	English and Spanish
Present Job	Concierge desk clerk (here at Mount Royal)
Skills	Typing
Previous Work	Bell person
Personality	Quiet and shy
Comments	Was late for interview but seemed knowledgeable. Good work record

Name	Joe Lanfranchi
Age	58
Education	Didn't complete school
Languages	English
Present Job	Concierge for the past three years
Skills	Computer skills
Previous Work	Porter, bell person, cashier, desk clerk
Personality	Loud but friendly and cheerful
Comments	Good at paperwork, according to references

Name	John Waterman
Age	38
Education	Didn't complete catering college
Languages	English and intermediate Japanese
Present Job	Porter/desk clerk in Mount Royal, New York
Skills	Typing and driving
Previous Work	Three years in Japan as international courier, but previously unemployed for 5 years
Personality	Calm but not very confident
Comments	Didn't seem sure what the job entails

10 Activity

What qualities and qualifications do you think are needed to work in (a) the Housekeeping section and (b) the Maintenance section of a hotel?

Divide into two groups, **A** and **B**. Group **A** should read text **1**. Group **B** should read text **2**.

As you read, make notes about the following:

a qualities needed
b duties
c experience and training

When you have finished, exchange information with a member of the other group.

Which job would you prefer?

1

Housekeeping

Are you smart? Intelligent? Don't mind hard work? Interested in looking after guests and helping to make their stay enjoyable? You could be just who we're looking for, to join our hotel housekeeping staff.

As a member of the Housekeeping team, you may be given responsibility for one of the bedroom areas. After the guests have checked out, you will then change beds, towels, etc. and generally ensure that everything is clean and tidy.

Housekeeping, however, is not just about cleaning bedrooms, but also keeping every public area pleasant, clean, and tidy for others to relax and work in. You may find you have to arrange flowers, displays of materials, publications, and be responsible for ensuring stocks are up-to-date whether in a linen room or a mini-bar. Other duties you may be involved in could be vacuuming, polishing, and tidying other areas in the building. You will certainly need to spend time checking everything is in place.

Whether you work at a hotel, motel, bed and breakfast, conference or holiday centre, or a tourist attraction, your guests will judge their accommodation by its appearance. Clean rooms and good service enhance any accommodation and make your guests return.

No previous experience is required and most of your training will be on the job, with extra in-house training given by the company's training personnel.

Opportunities

2

Maintenance

Just think how many things need doing around the house. Now imagine how many more there are in a large hotel – or a leisure theme park! Lighting, heating, plumbing, carpentry, even gardening needs taking care of. Courtesy cars and staff buses need driving and many large hotels need grounds staff to look after their golf-courses and keep them in tip-top condition. Whilst some smaller hotels use outside contractors, most larger hotels, motorway sites, and leisure parks employ their own specialized support staff. Because guests and visitors expect everything to work perfectly, maintenance and support staff must be available 24 hours a day. This means you will probably have to work shifts and some weekends.

Many people start in these jobs by applying direct. To get a job as a plumber, carpenter, or electrician you can start as an apprentice, no experience is needed, and you will be trained on the job.

If your interest is in gardening or green-keeping, again no experience is necessary to start, but you will need to have a real love of horticulture, and enjoy working out of doors.

Whenever people travel on long journeys they need to stop for a break. At the sites where they stop, more specialist support staff are needed to look after them – car and coach parks need to be controlled, cloakrooms supervised, and all amenities kept clean and tidy. Obviously, every one of these jobs is different, but they all have one thing in common – looking after the customer!

11 Vocabulary

answerable to p. 153 (tapescript), responsible to

apprentice p. 40, someone who works for a skilled employer for a fixed period in return for being taught the skills necessary for that job

bargaining p. 34, discussing prices, etc. to get a result that is to your own advantage

candidate p. 38, person who applies for a job or wants to be elected to a particular position

carpenter p. 40, person whose job is making or repairing wooden things

chambermaids p. 31, women whose job it is to clean and tidy hotel bedrooms

clientele p. 34, group of customers or guests

comes under the remit of p. 154 (tapescript), is the responsibility of

command of p. 37, knowledge of

courteous p. 36, polite

day-to-day p. 32, planning for only one day at a time

dealings with sb p. 154 (tapescript), relations with sb, especially in business

delegates p. 37, people who have been chosen to attend a conference

dispatch of luggage p. 154 (tapescript), sending luggage

duties p. 34, tasks that must be done

enhance p. 40, improve

entails p. 39, involves

external to p. 36, outside

heavy workload p. 34, a lot of work to do

horticulture p. 40, art of growing flowers, fruit and vegetables

hoteliers p. 34, people who own or manage hotels

in-house training p. 40, training given in the hotel by the hotel staff

liaise p. 37, communicate and co-operate

log-book p. 36, official written record of guests' queries and requests

maintenance staff p. 40, people whose job is to keep things in good condition or good working order

onward travel p. 154 (tapescript), going on from one destination to another

outside contractors p. 40, firms used by other firms (instead of their own staff) to do jobs under contract

overall vision p. 153 (tapescript), general objectives

personal touch p. 34, personal service

personnel p. 31, department that deals with employees

plumber p. 40, person whose job is to fit and repair water-pipes, tanks, etc. in buildings

profitable p. 153 (tapescript), that makes a profit

queries p. 154 (tapescript), questions

skills p. 38, abilities you need to do a job well

smart p. 40, neat and well-dressed

staff p. 34, employees

tip p. 32, a small amount of money given for good service

tip-top condition p. 40, perfect condition

turnover of stock p. 34, rate at which goods are used

use his discretion p. 153, decide himself

work record p. 39, things known about the work someone has done in the past

work shifts p. 33, take turns working with other people

workaholic p. 34, someone who cannot stop working

4 Reservations and check-in

1 Word study

Hotels use a variety of documents to deal with guests. Computerized and manual systems often have the same functions, although the names are sometimes different.

Here is a list of records used by a typical hotel front office:

1 Hotel Register
2 Reservation Form or Card
3 Reservation Diary or Daily Arrival List
4 Reservation Chart
5 Room Status Board
6 Guest Index
7 Guest History

Can you match the documents above with these definitions?

a Provides a visual record of all reservations for a period and shows at a glance rooms reserved and those remaining to be sold.
b Lists all current guests in alphabetical order with their room numbers and provides an additional quick point of reference in larger hotels.
c Standardizes the details of each booking, forms the top sheet of any documents relating to it, and enables a speedy reference to any individual case.
d Records all previous visits to the hotel for any individual and contains important statistical reservation and revenue data.

e Shows all rooms by room number and floor, and gives the current and projected status of all rooms on a particular day, with details of occupation.

f Records all bookings by date of arrival and shows all arrivals for a particular day at a glance.

g Records all arrivals as they occur and gives details of all current and past guests.

Which of these records are unlikely to be found in (i) a manual system, and (ii) a computerized system?

2 Listening

Listen to these two callers phoning the Hotel Melissa to make reservations. Complete the information in the chart below:

	Caller 1	Caller 2
Name of guest(s)		
Arrival date		
No. of nights		
Room type		
Company/Individual		
Stayed before		
Method of payment		
Credit card no.		
Address		
Reservation no.		
Special requests		

3 Language study   Pronunciation of letters

Often when making reservations or filling in forms, names have to be
spelt out loud. How good is your pronunciation of letters?

As a pronunciation check, list the letters of the alphabet according to their
vowel sounds. The first three have been done for you.

/eɪ/ (grey)	/iː/ (green)	/e/ (red)	/aɪ/ (white)	/əʊ/ (yellow)	/uː/ (blue)	/ɑː/ (dark)
A	B	___	___	___	___	___
___	C	___	___		___	
___	___	___			___	
	___	___				
	___	___				
	___	___				
	___					

Spell your full name to your partner.

Think of three people you know (family or friends), and spell their names
to your partner as quickly as possible.

Short answers

Look at how the callers give short answers to the questions of the
reservations clerk:

Have you stayed with us before?
▶ *No,* **I haven't.**
Will you be paying by credit card?
▶ *Yes,* **I will.**
You have an account with us, don't you?
▶ *Yes,* **we do.**

Using short answers, answer the questions:

a Do you have a reservation? (No)
b Is it just for the one night? (Yes)
c Would you like one of our Executive rooms? (Yes)
d Is there one available on the ground floor? (No)
e Will you be staying tomorrow as well? (No)
f Is that a company booking? (Yes)
g Have they confirmed their booking? (Yes)
h Do you have a room with a view? (Yes)

Tag questions

Notice the way we use tag questions to ask for confirmation:

▶ *It was Miss King, **wasn't it?***
▶ *You have an account with us, **don't you?***
▶ *But the guests haven't stayed with us before, **have they?***

Now add tag questions to the following statements:

a There isn't a doctor in the hotel, _____?

b You wanted to pay in cash, _____?

c You haven't spoken to the duty manager yet, _____?

d We couldn't have a receipt for that, _____?

e It's more expensive in high season, _____?

f You're settling by credit card, _____?

g We can sign the agreement today, _____?

h They're not postponing the conference, _____?

4 Reading

'Lodgistix' is a computer software company which specializes in providing computer software for the hotel industry. You are going to read part of the information brochure about their Reservation and Front Office Systems.

1 Read the text which follows and match each paragraph with one of the summary sentences below. Don't worry if you can't understand every word – just try to understand the general meaning.

a You will quickly be able to find out if a guest has stayed before and use this information.

b You can change the system to suit your particular hotel.

c Your marketing department will be able to use the information in the Reservation System.

d Your employees will find the system easy to use.

e You will be able to process guests quickly when they arrive (and when they leave) by allocating suitable rooms immediately.

f You can use detailed statistical analysis of the guests to help increase profits.

g Your guests will get a better service and you will get a bigger profit.

LODGISTIX presents
LANmark Property Management System – the next generation!

Enter a world of incredible speed and knowledge!

Written by hotel people for hotel people, and especially for network technology, LANmark is amazingly intuitive in use. Seamless integration of modules puts all your hotel services together in a powerful computer system that is both flexible and unlimited.

Reservations & Front Office

1 The LANmark Reservation System provides total flexibility in tailoring the system to meet each individual client's needs.

2 There is greater potential to increase revenues by use of up-to-the-minute statistics from market segments, sources of business, nationality codes, corporate client details, guest history records, and property totals.

3 The Reservation System utilizes help keys and windowing features throughout, enabling the reservationist easily to identify and act on information displayed. The use of colours is an important feature further aiding the operator. All informational and screen formats have been designed for fast, accurate, and complete reservations processing.

4 On reservation entry, a search of matching Guest History names can be made quickly and easily, greatly reducing the booking time for future reservations. The Guest History record contains important statistical reservation and revenue data clearly showing the last time the guest stayed, the total number of stays to date, and total spent. Unlimited guest folios can also be stored including full transaction details.

5 The Reservation System allows for the creation of word processing merge files for all or selected Guest History masters, and is an important marketing tool. Both the sales and marketing departments can access this information through management and password controls.

6 The Lodgistix LANmark Front Office System has been designed to improve guest services and maximize profits.

7 There is provision for quick individual and group reservation check-in and check-out to minimize guest waiting-time. Registration cards can be printed prior to arrival in a batch print run or on arrival upon request. At registration, the receptionist can auto-assign a room number or display the room rack to select a room number that meets the guest's requirements. Room selection can be by room descriptions, complex room type, or rate code to give maximum flexibility in allocating the required rooms.

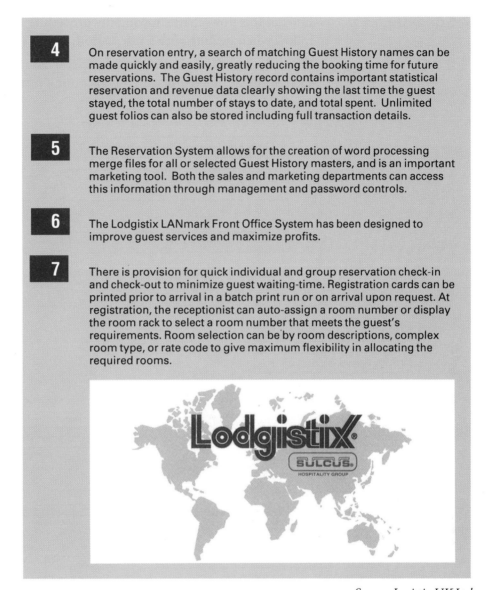

Source: Logistix UK Ltd

2 Find words in the text which mean:

   a a set of computers connected in order to send and share information
   b divisions on a computer screen to show separate pieces of information
   c the front glass surface of a computer monitor
   d the style in which information is displayed
   e information (for processing or storing)
   f files that combine different information from different sources into a single document
   g obtain stored information from a computer's memory
   h a secret group of letters or numbers which must be used by a person before they can operate a computer system
   i a single operation to produce a large group of similar documents

5 Speaking

Look at this flow-chart showing the procedure that hotel staff should follow when dealing with a reservation.

Write down on a separate sheet of paper what the hotel employee says at each of the numbered places, then act out a conversation with a partner.

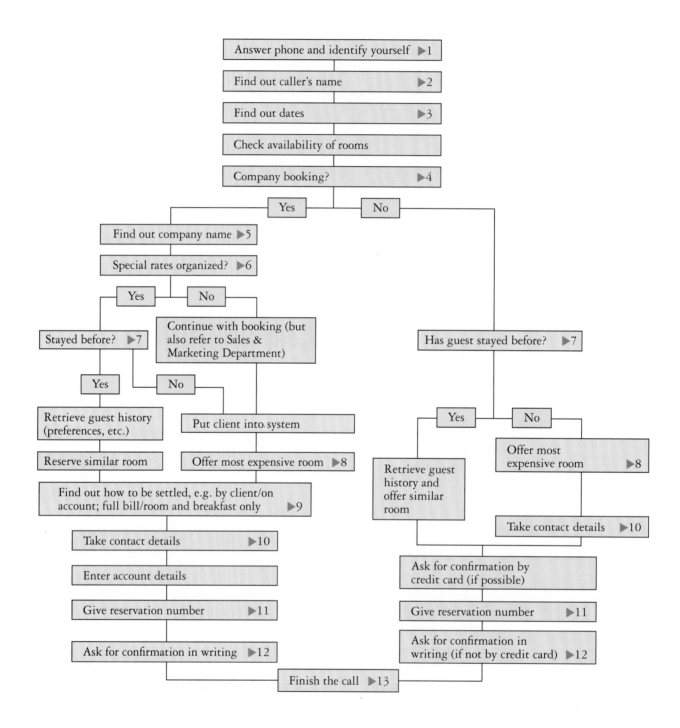

6 Reading

For most hotels, fax reservations are the most common. Read this example of a fax reservation and complete the chart below:

C T L COMFORT TOURS LONDON

FAX MESSAGE

Date:	13th March 199__
From:	Kate James
To:	Melissa Hotel

Attention:　　Reservations　　　　No. of pages:　1

Could you please reserve a double room with private bath for Mr and Mrs Charles Davies? They will be arriving on 18th April and staying for 3 nights (departing on the morning of 21st April).

It is their 25th wedding anniversary, so could you arrange for champagne and flowers to be placed in the room?

Look forward to receiving your confirmation, with exact cost, by return.

Regards

Name of guest(s)　　　　_____

Number of guests　　　　_____

Room(s) required　　　　_____

Dates　　　　　　　　　_____

Special requirements　　_____

---

7 Writing

Reply to the reservation by fax, asking for any additional information you require.

Melissa Hotel

●

FAX MESSAGE

From:　　　　　　　　　　　　　　Date:

To:　　　　　　　　　　　　　　　No. of pages:

Attention:

---

8 Listening

1 Below are some extracts from a conversation between a receptionist and a guest checking in without a reservation. Put them in the order (from 1 to 10) in which you think you will hear them.

a ☐ Would you like an Executive at £125 or a Standard at £95?

b ☐ And may I take your home address, please?

c ☐ It's room 760 on the seventh floor.

d ☐ Hello.

e ☐ And the name, sir, is . . . ?

f ☐ Here's your credit card, passport, and here's your key.

g ☐ This is your registration card. Can you just check through the details, please?

h ☐ Just the one night?

i ☐ Because you're not a British citizen, I'll require your passport in order to complete the registration.

j ☐ How will you be settling your account, sir?

2 Now listen to a real check-in conversation to see if your suggested order is the same.

9 Speaking

Working in pairs, invent some details for yourself and check in at your partner's hotel, following the check-in procedure above for people without reservations.

Use the details from the fax reservation and reply in *6 Reading* to act out the conversation at check-in when a reservation has been made.

10 Activity

1 Divide into groups of three or four. Each group should do two things:

   a Write a list of ten rooms which remain unbooked in your hotel for tonight. Each room should have an advantage and a disadvantage.

   Example:
   Room 106
   Advantage = lovely sea view
   Disadvantage = noisy because above the bar

   b Write a list of ten guests (singles or couples) who have reservations for tonight. Write a brief profile of each guest and make a note of their preferences (they do not need to match the ten rooms).

   Example:
   Elderly couple who want a quiet room near the lift.

2 Exchange your list of guests (but not your room list) with another group. Try to fit the guests into the rooms on your list so that as far as possible everyone gets what they want.

   At the end, show your solution to the other groups.

11 Activity

Divide into two groups, **A** and **B**.

A
You are computer company representatives. You will be trying to persuade a hotel manager to buy your computer system. Prepare a product presentation. What features does your system have? How will it help the hotel? Use the information from earlier in this unit if you want, but make sure the system is your own.

B
You are hotel managers. You are thinking of buying a new computer system for your hotel. What do you want the new system to be able to do? Prepare a list of questions to ask the computer company representative.

In pairs, act out the conversation between the computer company representative and the hotel manager.

At the end report back to your group about how successful/satisfied you were.

12 Vocabulary

aiding p. 46, helping

allocate a room p. 155 (tapescript), decide which room a guest will stay in

confirmation p. 48, agreeing to a booking already made

corporate client p. 46, client which is a company rather than an individual

flexibility p. 46, ability to adapt to different conditions

have a preference for p. 156 (tapescript), prefer

integration p. 46, combining various parts

market segments p. 46, particular parts of the market

manual p. 42, done by hand

matching p. 46, the same as

modules p. 46, units of a computer program that have a particular function

potential p. 46, possibility of being developed or used

prior to p. 47, before

process guests p. 46, complete all the official transactions necessary for guests to stay

provision for sth p. 47, preparation that has been made in case sth happens

reducing p. 46, making smaller

refer to sb p. 48, send to sb for advice or action

require p. 50, need, **requirement** p. 49, thing needed, **meet sb's requirements** p. 47, be what is needed

reservationist p. 46, reservation clerk

retrieve p. 48, get or find again

revenues p. 46, income

room rack p. 47, board containing cards showing the details of the rooms in the hotel

settling your account p. 50, paying your bill

software p. 45, computer data and programs

statistics p. 46, collection of information shown in numbers, *adj* **statistical** p. 42

tailoring sth to sb's needs p. 46, adapting sth for sb

take sb's contact details p. 48, write down sb's name, address, telephone number, etc.

transaction p. 46, piece of business conducted (especially between two people)

up-to-the-minute p. 46, including the most recent information

utilizes p. 46, uses

5   Hotel and restaurant services

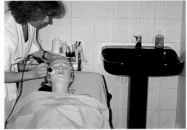

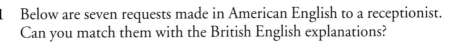

1 Word study

1 Below are seven requests made in American English to a receptionist. Can you match them with the British English explanations?

1 'Where are the rest-rooms?'
2 'Where can I find a drug-store to get some band-aid?'
3 'Can you get gas on the freeways?'
4 'Can I make a reservation for the fall?'
5 'My wife left her purse in the elevator at the subway station.'
6 'Can we have some cookies and candy for the kids sent up to the room?'
7 'We can't turn the faucet on.'

a He needs to buy some plasters at a chemist.
b He wants to make a reservation for the autumn.
c His wife left her handbag in the lift at the underground station.
d There's something wrong with the tap.
e He wants to know where the toilets are.
f He wants to know if he can buy petrol on the motorway.
g They want some biscuits and sweets in their room for the children.

2   Can you write the British English for the following American English words?

US	UK	US	UK
a traveler's check	_____	**e** closet	_____
b downtown	_____	**f** garbage/trash	_____
c vacation	_____	**g** diaper	_____
d potato chips	_____		

2 Reading

Read these two menus and fill in the gaps with the following words:

bread, fresh, garnish, served, cheese, home-made, spicy, seasoned, choice, sweet, sauce, coated, creamy, liqueur, selection, wrapped, roasted

MENU

Homemade Leek and Potato Soup
Hot and tasty combination of fresh leeks
and potato ¹_____ with fresh herbs

Crudités with Garlic Mayonnaise
Crunchy fresh vegetables served with
a tasty garlic mayonnaise dip

Melon and Prawn Cocktail
Delicate mixture of fresh melon and juicy
prawns with salad ²_____
,

Chicken Liver Pâté
Home-made chicken liver pâté served
with melba toast and a crisp side salad

....

CHEF'S SPECIAL DISH Chicken Kiev
Supreme of chicken crammed with garlic
butter ³_____ in fresh breadcrumbs

Roast Leg of Pork with Apple Sauce
Prime leg of pork ⁴_____ and carved to
order, served with home-made fresh
Bramley apple sauce

Beef Madras with Rice
Hot and ⁵_____ oriental curry served
with sambols and rice

**Fillet of Haddock in Breadcrumbs
with Tartare Sauce**
Fresh fillet of haddock coated in home-made
breadcrumbs and served with
⁶_____ tartare sauce

**Peas
Broccoli with Almonds
Lyonnaise Potatoes
Sauté Potatoes**

....

Fresh Fruit Salad
Seasonal fresh fruit salad in a fresh
orange juice. This is offered with a
⁷_____ of natural yoghurt or fresh cream

Apple and Honey Pie with Custard Sauce
Freshly-baked apple drizzled
with honey and served under a
crust of ⁸_____ pastry

GOURMET MENU

Les délices de Grison
Air cured beef and ham from the Engadine

La crème aux amandes
A ⁹ almond soup

Les escargots en chausson
Six snails perfumed with garlic and ¹⁰ in pastry.

✳

La petite salade
A mixed garden-¹¹ salad

Le sorbet au marc de champagne
Sorbet with marc de champagne

✳

Les mignons de porc à l'orange
Medallions of pork in a spicy orange ¹² served with pilaff rice

L'émincé de veau zurichois
Thin slices of veal and mushrooms in a creamy sauce ¹³
with rösti potatoes

La mousse de saumon 'ciboulette' et la bouquetière de légumes et le riz sauvage
A light salmon mousse in a chive sauce served with a ¹⁴ of
vegetables and wild rice

La fondue valaisanne
Dip crusty cubes of ¹⁵ into bubbling ¹⁶ and wine and
enjoy the taste of Switzerland

✳

Le gâteau aux noisettes
Hazelnut cream gâteau

Soufflé glacé au Grand Marnier
A favourite ice cream soufflé flavoured with Grand Marnier ¹⁷

Le parfait glacé à la nougatine
Home-made nougat-flavoured ice parfait

✳

Le café et les truffes
Coffee and home-made truffles

Source: The Swiss Centre, London

3 Listening   Listen to some people ordering food from the menus shown. What do they order?

	Dialogue 1		Dialogue 2		Dialogue 3	
	Man	Woman	Man	Woman	Man	Woman
Starter	____	____	____	____	____	____
	____	____	____	____	____	____
Main course	____	____	____	____	____	____
	____	____	____	____	____	____
Dessert	____	____	____	____	____	____
	____	____	____	____	____	____

4 Language study   Intentions and spontaneous decisions

Look at how we talk about things that we have already decided:

▶ ***I'm going to have** the fondue. It's delicious here.*

Look at how we make decisions at the moment of speaking:

▶ *In that case, **I'll have** the pork medallions.*

In the following exercise, put the verb into the correct form using either *will* or *going to*.

Example:
'What would you like, tea or coffee?' *'Oh, I'll have coffee, please.'*

a 'Have you written that letter yet?' 'Oh, no – I forgot. I _____ (do) it now.'

b 'I've decided to buy a new car.' 'Oh, have you? What sort _____ (you/buy)?'

c 'Has Susan got any plans, now she's finished college?' 'Oh, yes. She _____ (look) for a job in hotel management.'

d 'I can't remember how to retrieve a customer's guest history on the computer.' 'Oh, don't worry. It's quite easy. I _____ (show) you.'

e 'Have you finalized arrangements with that tour operator?' 'Yes, we _____ (sign) the contract with them tomorrow.'

f 'I'm afraid there is no chicken tonight.' 'OK. We _____ (have) the beef.'

g 'We haven't got any more coffee.' 'Haven't we? OK, I _____ (ask) someone to buy some more.'

Making requests

Look at the way the people in the restaurant asked for things:

▶ ***Can you*** *bring us a bottle of water, please?*
▶ ***Could you*** *change mine, please?*
▶ ***Could we possibly*** *order, please?*
▶ ***Do you think you could*** *bring us the wine list, . . . ?*

Now ask similar questions using the verbs in brackets.

a You don't know the telephone number of a caller. (give)
b You didn't hear a customer's surname. (repeat)
c You don't know how to spell the name of a town. (spell)
d You want to know if there are any vegetarians in a group. (tell)
e You are not sure what time a guest is arriving. (confirm)
f You want to check how many people there are in a group. (tell)

5 Speaking

1 Complete the waiter's half of the dialogue, using the prompts in brackets. Then act out the dialogue in pairs.

WAITER: (Evening.)
CUSTOMER: Good evening.
WAITER: (Two?)
CUSTOMER: Yes, please.
WAITER: (Aperitif?)
CUSTOMER: No, thanks.
WAITER: (Menu.)
CUSTOMER: Thanks.

WAITER: (Order?)
CUSTOMER: Well, I'm not quite sure what to have.
WAITER: (The veal?)
CUSTOMER: All right. I'll have that.
WAITER: (To start?)
CUSTOMER: Almond soup, please.
WAITER: (Wine?)
CUSTOMER: Yes. A bottle of house white, please.

WAITER: (All right?)
CUSTOMER: Yes, thanks. Delicious.
WAITER: (Dessert?)
CUSTOMER: Hazelnut gâteau for me, I think.
WAITER: (Coffee?)
CUSTOMER: Yes, thanks. That would be nice.

2 Now use the waiter language and the menus to act out the conversations between the waiter and the guests in a hotel restaurant.

6 Reading　　　**1**　Where exactly in a hotel would you see these notices and signs?

a **RESERVED**

b **FIRE EXIT**

c PLEASE VACATE YOUR ROOM BY 12 NOON

d **We accept...** *VISA, MASTERCARD, AMERICAN EXPRESS*

e **VEHICLES LEFT AT OWNER'S RISK**

f **IF FOUND PLEASE RETURN TO:** *MELISSA HOTEL PO BOX 969 LARNACA, CYPRUS*

g **PLEASE DO NOT DISTURB**

h The management and staff are here to ensure that you have a pleasant stay. Please call reception if you have any further requirements.

i **IN CASE OF FIRE ... BREAK GLASS AND PRESS BELL**

j **Dial 9 for an outside line**

k **PRESS BUTTON TO OPERATE** ☞

l *Please service my room*

2　Read the following extract from the 'Welcome Information' notes placed in the rooms at the Forte Crest Hotel in Gloucester. Complete the gaps with these words:

advance, advisable, arrangements, attractions, available, hired, loan, pleased, programmes, returned, served, vacate

▼ Comments

The Duty Manager will be **1**_____ to hear any suggestions, or to help with any problems or difficulties you may have.

▼ Departure

Please **2**_____ your room by midday on the day of departure.

▼ Dinner

Served in the Berkeley Restaurant daily: Monday - Sunday 7.00 - 10.00 pm (last orders).

It is always **3**_____ to book to be sure of a table. Reservations can be made through Reception.

'Late night platters' are available, **4**_____ in your room if arriving after restaurant hours, provided they are booked in **5**_____ at Reception.

▼ Dry cleaning and laundry

A laundry bag, list and tariff are in your dressing-table drawer. All items placed with Reception by 9.00 am will be **6**_____ the same day. This service is not **7**_____ at weekends.

▼ Entertainment

We hold current brochures for major local **8**_____ , and Reception will be pleased to advise on local cinema and theatre **9**_____ .

▼ Games

A chess set, draughts and children's games, etc. are available on **10**_____ from Reception.

▼ Golf

There is an excellent 18-hole golf-course locally, at the Cotswold Hills Golf Club. Equipment can be **11**_____ if necessary. Please contact Reception who will make **12**_____ for you.

3   Suggest headings for these items from the 'Welcome Information' notes:

▼ **a** _____

An electric iron and ironing-board are available on loan by contacting Reception.

▼ **b** _____

Please contact Reception who will gladly book a taxi for you.

▼ **c** _____

The switchboard has the facility to allow guests to listen into their children's room from any house phone. Please ring Reception for details.

▼ **d** _____

Provided in a special folder in the dressing-table drawer.

▼ **e** _____

May be ordered from Reception and will be delivered to your room in the morning.

▼ **f** _____

The management cannot accept responsibility for guests' effects left on the premises, but a valuable item may be deposited for safe keeping against a receipt signed by the Manager or a member of the Reception staff. The receipt must be retained as it will be required as the authority for the item to be withdrawn from deposit.

7 Listening   Listen to these conversations between guests and Reception. Complete
the notes below.

From	Room	Message/Request	Contact
1			
2			
3			

8 Writing   The receptionist has received the following messages in the last hour. Can
you expand the notes into full sentences?

> 1. Smith 106 champagne x 2 a.s.a.p.
>
> 2. Mrs Kurz 110 early call 6 a.m.
>   + taxi airport (tomorrow).
>
> 3. Jane Peters 196 wants check out day early (prepare
>   bill): room available if needed.
>
> 4. Message for Otto Post (room?) from Jurgen (friend)
>   - arriving airport 9 a.m. tomorrow - can he meet?
>
> 5. Mrs Kempf (204) message for husband (leave at
>   reception) will meet in restaurant at 8pm.

Example:
*Mr Smith in Room 106 would like a bottle of champagne and two glasses
brought to his room as soon as possible.*

9 Activity

One of the most important services for hotel guests is the food and drink service. In a large hotel this is organized in what is called 'the food and beverage cycle' and involves a considerable number of staff.

There are five sections to the cycle:

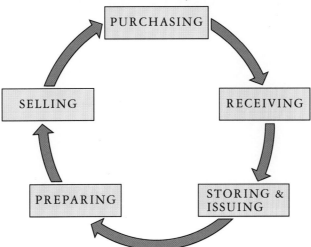

In small groups, match the job titles below with the job descriptions.

1	head chef	a	sets and clears the tables
2	storeman	b	buys food and drinks, deals with suppliers
3	wine waiter	c	welcomes the clients to the restaurant, deals with complaints
4	receiving officer	d	looks after one section of the kitchen
5	commis chef	e	checks deliveries, arranges transfer to stores
6	head waiter	f	cooks food and is training to be a chef
7	maître d'	g	arranges staff's work in the dining-room
8	purchasing officer	h	plans menus, trains and supervises kitchen staff
9	chef de partie	i	serves customers, takes orders, brings food
10	bus boy	j	helps supervise kitchen staff
11	sous chef/under chef	k	looks after stock, gives it to various departments
12	waiter/waitress	l	takes drinks orders, advises on wines

Now put the jobs into the relevant sections of the chart below.

Food and Beverage Cycle

Purchasing	Receiving	Storing and Issuing	Preparing	Selling

10 Activity

Four people, Jeff, Pierre, Susanna, and Helen, have ordered breakfast, but their orders are jumbled. Can you work out who ordered what? Each person ordered three food items, and at least one drink.

	Drinks		Food items		
	Juice	Hot drink	1	2	3
Jeff					
Pierre					
Susanna					
Helen					

a Jeff has ordered orange juice and coffee.

b Helen wants croissants.

c Everyone wants orange juice except one person, who wants grapefruit juice and tea.

d Everybody wants either eggs or croissants, but nobody wants both.

e One man and one woman have ordered eggs.

f The woman who wants fried eggs wants orange juice and no hot drink.

g The man who is having coffee does not want croissants.

h The man who wants croissants also wants orange juice and hot chocolate.

i Both croissant-eaters want butter, but only the woman wants jam.

j The person with no hot drink has ordered sausages and mushrooms.

k The person who wants fruit yoghurt does not drink coffee.

l The person who wants scrambled eggs has also ordered toast and butter.

11 Vocabulary

aperitif p. 57, alcoholic drink taken before a meal

baked p. 55, cooked by dry heat in an oven, e.g. bread, cakes

carved p. 55, cut (meat)

coated in p. 55, covered in

crisp p. 55, firm and fresh

crunchy p. 55, fresh and crisp; making a sharp sound when bitten into

crust p. 55, hard outer surface

current p. 59, in use at the moment

deposited p. 59, given to sb to be kept in a safe place

dessert p. 56, sweet dish eaten as final course in a meal

dressing-table p. 59, bedroom table with mirror and drawers, used especially by women when they dress, make up, etc.

equipment p. 59, thing(s) needed for a particular purpose

facility p. 59, ability

folder p. 59, cover for holding loose paper, etc.

garlic p. 54, small plant like an onion with a strong taste and smell

garnish p. 54, vegetable, herb, etc., used to decorate a dish or add to its flavour

herbs p. 55, plants whose leaves are used for flavouring food

juicy p. 55, containing a lot of juice and being enjoyable to eat

laundry p. 59, clothes, sheets, etc., that need to be washed; place where this is done

liqueur p. 54, strong (usually sweet) alcoholic spirit, drunk in small quantities especially after a meal

pastry p. 54, mixture of flour, fat, and water, baked in an oven and used to cover pies, etc.

petrol p. 53, liquid used as fuel for cars

plasters p. 53, small pieces of fabric or plastic that can be stuck to the skin to cover a small wound or cut

platters p. 59, large flat dishes with a selection of food

retained p. 59, kept

roasted p. 54, cooked in an oven

seasonal p. 55, varying with the seasons

seasoned p. 54, flavoured

slices p. 54, thin, wide, flat pieces cut off an item of food

snails p. 54, small, slow-moving animals with a shell

spicy p. 54, flavoured with spice; strong-tasting because of high pepper or chilli content

starter p. 56, first course of a meal

supervise p. 61, watch sb to make sure they are doing their job properly

switchboard p. 59, central telephone panel

tap p. 53, thing that controls the flow of water in a bath, basin, etc.

tariff p. 59, list of fixed charges

tasty p. 55, having a strong and pleasant flavour; appetizing

vacate p. 58, leave

valuable p. 59, worth a lot of money

vegetarians p. 57, people who do not eat meat

6 Money matters

1 Reading

1 What items would you expect to find on a hotel bill? Continue this list:

room charge (per night)

meals

phone calls

_____

_____

_____

_____

_____

_____

2 Look at this example of a bill for a guest staying at the Royal York Hotel. Answer the questions which follow.

The Royal York Hotel

Station Road
York
YO2 2AA

Telephone (0904) 653681.
Telex 57912.
Fax: (0904) 623503.

Page No: 1
Folio No: 9182
Name: Mrs Townsend
Address: OWN ACCOUNT
Nationality: GB

Room: 504
Room Rate: 116.00 (D)
Arrived: 26 October
Departed: 28 October
No. Persons: 3

Date	Outlet	Description	Charges	Total
26 Oct	Lounge Bar	S	2.65	
26 Oct	Lounge Bar	S	7.35	
26 Oct	Rose Room Drink	S	3.90	
26 Oct	Rose Room Wine	S	11.25	
26 Oct	Rose Room Dinner	S	3.50	
26 Oct	Dinner Bed & Bfas	S	116.00	
26 Oct	Newspapers: Paid O	E	.30	
27 Oct	Dinner Bed & Bfas	S	116.00	
27 Oct	Rose Room Wine	S	12.50	273.45

a How many people were staying?
b What was the room number?
c How many nights did they stay?
d What was the daily room rate, and what did this include?
e What was *not* included in the room rate?
f What extras did they buy?
g How did they pay?

2 Listening **1** Look at the list below, then listen to three dialogues involving money which take place in a hotel. Each dialogue is about one of the following situations. Write the number of the dialogue by the situation you hear.

a ☐ paying the bill in the restaurant
b ☐ buying goods from a hotel shop
c ☐ checking in
d ☐ changing money
e ☐ checking out
f ☐ leaving a tip

2 In the dialogues, several questions are asked. Listen to the cassette again and complete the questions below.

Dialogue 1

a How would you like _____?
b Could you just _____ here, please?
c How much do you _____?

Dialogue 2

d Would you just like to _____ it _____?
e Can you tell me what this _____ is for?
f Do you _____ Visa?

Dialogue 3

g Can you tell me what the _____ is?
h Cash or _____?
i Is _____ charged on that?

Which questions are asked by the guest and which by the hotel employee?

3 Language study Using numbers

Look at the way numbers and figures are used in the dialogues. Compare the spoken form with the written form on the right.

'That'll be thirty-seven pounds twenty, please . . .'	(£37.20)
'Room four oh eight.'	(408)
'Two hundred divided by one point four equals one hundred and forty-two pounds eighty-six . . .'	(200÷1.4 = £142.86)
'. . . less two pounds commission . . . comes to one hundred and forty pounds eighty-six pence.'	(−£2.00 = £140.86)

1 Now match these figures with the spoken sentences which follow.

1 £2.50   5 $100 bill
2 $2,216   6 Room 504: £273.45
3 £1.00 = $1.86   7 4 × $4.25 = $17
4 £24 + 15% service = £27.60   8 $100 − 10% = $90

a We're currently exchanging at one dollar eighty-six to the pound.
b The total charge for the group is two thousand, two hundred and sixteen dollars.
c I gave you a hundred-dollar bill!
d That will be two pounds fifty, please.
e One hundred dollars less ten per cent commission makes ninety dollars.
f Four times four dollars twenty-five is seventeen dollars in all.
g The bill for room five oh four comes to two hundred and seventy-three pounds forty-five (pence).
h Twenty-four pounds plus fifteen per cent service equals twenty-seven pounds sixty.

2 Read these amounts to a partner and get them to make the final calculation.

a £2.50 + £4.15 =
b 10% of $150 =
c 5 × £14 =
d £206 + £2,314 =
e $16.95 × 2 =
f $1000 − 10% =
g £60 + 15% =
h $4,396 + 3,221 =

Make up some of your own and read them to your partner.

The Passive

Look at these examples of the Passive from the dialogues:

▶ *It can **be added** to your bill.*
(= We can add it to your bill.)
▶ *I can arrange for them to **be sent**.*
(= I can arrange for someone to send them.)
▶ *Those papers **were sent** to 703.*
(= Someone sent those papers to 703.)
▶ *I've **been given** the wrong bill.*
(= Someone has given me the wrong bill.)
▶ *Is commission **charged** on that?*
(= Do you charge commission on that?)

The passive is often used when:

a the thing happening is more important than the person or thing doing it (the agent).
b the agent is unknown or unnecessary.
c a more formal style is required.

Transform these active sentences into passive sentences.

Example:
They are building an extension next year.
An extension is being built next year.

a We add a service charge to your bill.
b The housekeeping department hasn't changed the sheets since last week.
c They delivered the wrong newspapers to room 703.
d Someone has stolen my passport!
e As I turned round, the waiter was pouring the wine.
f We expect guests to check out before twelve noon.

4 Word study

1 Match these words with the pictures underneath:

1 receipt	5 traveller's cheque
2 cheque (British bank)	6 credit card
3 cash (notes)	7 bill
4 cash (coins)	8 Eurocheque

2 a Which ones are methods of payment?
   b Think of an item or service which can be paid for by each.
   c What are the advantages and disadvantages of the different methods of payment?

3 Here is a list of precautions that reception and sales staff should take when dealing with different methods of payment. Which method of payment should they be used with? Discuss with a partner.

   a check expiry date
   b compare signatures
   c watch client sign
   d write number on back
   e take imprint of card
   f hold up to light and examine
   g ask for passport or other identification
   h phone client's bank

4 Complete the text using the following words:

   check out, deposit, in advance, sales outlet, settle a bill, voucher

   ## Guest accounting

   Hotels operate complex systems of guest accounting. Rooms are not usually paid for ¹_____ . It is normal for guests to ²_____ only when they ³_____ of the hotel – although usually a ⁴_____ or credit card number is taken as security. A guest will probably buy a number of hotel services during his/her stay, for example, drinks in the bar, room service, and so on. These are either paid for at the time or added to the guest's final bill (in which case the ⁵_____ must issue a signed ⁶_____ to the accounts department).

   Source: S. Medlik: The Business of Hotels

5 Speaking

In pairs, **A** and **B**, act out the dialogue between a receptionist and a guest who is checking out. This is the guest's bill:

The Clinton Hotel

George Street, Bath, BA1 7AY

Telephone: (0225) 867246. Fax: (0225) 867201

Page No.	1	Room	309
Folio No.	–	Room rate	116.00 (D)
Name	W. Bridgeman	Arrived	15 Apr
Address	OWN ACCOUNT	Departed	16 Apr
Nationality	GB	No. Persons	2

Date	Item	Charge
15 Apr 199 _	Room	116.00
15 Apr 199 _	Phone	2.50
15 Apr 199 _	Room service	32.00
16 Apr 199 _	Newspaper	1.00
16 Apr 199 _	Mini-bar	12.50
Total		164.00

A

You are the receptionist. You've been warned about this guest before – he/she has caused problems at a lot of places in the hotel. Be prepared to explain some of the items, but you are sure the bill is correct – the phone system, for example, is automatic and cannot make mistakes. Don't forget to ask how the guest is going to pay. Be polite!

B

You are the guest. You are not happy with this bill so you want to query some of the items. For example, you didn't use the telephone and you only ordered a sandwich from room service. How do you want to pay?

Start the dialogue like this:

RECEPTIONIST: Good morning. How can I help you?
GUEST: I'd like to check out, please.
RECEPTIONIST: Certainly. What room are you in?
GUEST: . . .

6 Reading

Read this memo explaining the Grand Hotel's policy on room rates. Answer the questions which follow.

Memo

From: The General Manager   Date: September 5 199__

To: All Front Office staff   Subject: Pricing policy

GRAND HOTEL

It is clear that some clarification of our policy on pricing and room rates is needed.

BASIC RATES

We have a basic rate for all room types. However, it is common for different rates to be charged. This is because the Sales and Marketing Department negotiates special rates for different agents, corporate clients, and other clients.

The basic rates are:

Standard room: £80.00 (double)   Luxury/Executive Plus: £115.00 (double)   Suite: Individually priced

Standard discounts

Weekend rate (Fri/Sat or Sat/Sun): 15% discount
Weekly rate: seven nights for the price of five

Specially-negotiated rates

Most guests come as part of a tour, through a tour operator, or as a corporate guest. In this case a special rate will have been negotiated and will be on the computer for Reservations and the Front Office to access.

Free Sale Agents

Free Sale Agents are sent availability charts every two weeks. They sell rooms at an agreed rate (usually the corporate rate). They don't have to check with us, so administration costs are kept low.

Allocation Holders

Allocation Holders have a certain number of rooms which they agree to sell (usually at FIT rates). The customer pays them directly and they take commission and pass on what is left to the hotel.

For weekends they have the rooms on a 48-hour release (in other words the hotel can take them back by Thursday and resell).

If you have any more questions, please speak to the Reservations Manager or the Sales and Marketing Department.

---

1 a Who decides the rate for different agents?
   b When must a guest stay to get a 15% reduction?
   c Where does the hotel get most of its guests from?
   d Why does selling rooms through Free Sale Agents keep administration costs down?
   e What is the difference between a Free Sale Agent and an Allocation Holder?

2 Using the information in the memo, calculate the income for the hotel in each of these cases:

a Three couples staying for two nights (Friday and Saturday) in Standard rooms.

b One businessman staying in an Executive Plus room for three nights (not a corporate client).

c A group of ten corporate clients each staying in a separate room (Luxury) for one night. The Sales and Marketing Department has agreed a 20% discount with this company.

7 Listening

1 Listen to this interview with the Reservations Manager of the Grand Hotel, recorded a year after the memo was sent. As you listen, note the changes that have been made in the policy of the Grand Hotel regarding room rates.

2 Using the new information, calculate what the income for the hotel will now be in the three cases in *6 Reading*, **2** above.

8 Writing

Read this letter sent to the group of three couples mentioned in *6 Reading*, **2a**.

Seafront Villas Westbourne BN43 1H4

GRAND HOTEL

Tel: 0273 624999   Fax: 0273 624831

10th August 199__

Mr and Mrs Davies
16 Hill Street
London N16 1BV

Dear Mr and Mrs Davies

Thank you for your letter of 5th August regarding a possible reservation for three rooms for two nights for the weekend of 14th/15th October.

We can offer either our Luxury double room at £115 per night or our Standard double at £85. All our rooms have private bathrooms, television, tea- and coffee-making facilities, and other features designed to make your stay as comfortable as possible.

Furthermore, we are able to offer you a special 10% weekend discount on these rates. The total for the three doubles will therefore be £459 for the Standard rooms or £621 for the Luxury rooms.

I would be grateful if you could confirm your reservation as soon as possible and tell us which type of room you would prefer. We accept all major credit cards or, if you prefer, you can secure your reservation by sending a 25% deposit.

I look forward to hearing from you.

Yours sincerely

P Barnes

Peter Barnes
Reservations Manager

Now write a similar letter in answer to the enquiry in **2b** or **2c**. Use the updated information from *7 Listening* and follow this structure:

Paragraph 1: Thank the enquirer for their letter
Paragraph 2: Explain the basic room rate
Paragraph 3: Explain details of any discount you are able to offer
Paragraph 4: Ask for confirmation
Paragraph 5: Closing remark

9 Activity

1 Work in pairs. Complete columns 1 and 2 of this chart by looking at today's newspaper. Together, complete columns 3 and 4. You will need to set buying and selling rates for each currency, and decide whether you are going to charge commission.

	1	2	3	4
COUNTRY	CURRENCY	TODAY'S EXCHANGE RATE (to your currency)		
			Cash	
		Rate from paper	Your buying rate	Your selling rate
UK				
USA				
Japan				
Germany				
Greece				

2 Take turns to be **A** and **B**.

A
You work in the exchange office of a large hotel. Using the rates you have just set, answer the questions of the tourists who come to your office to change money.

B
You are a tourist. Choose one of the currencies and decide how much you have. Go round the class, visiting other students' exchange offices and trying to get the best rate. Act out the conversation.

Useful language:

Can you tell me the exchange rate for . . .?
I'd like to change these . . .
How many . . . will I get for . . .?
Does that include commission?

10 Activity

1   In groups discuss these questions:

   a   Have you ever been given a tip?
   b   What is the biggest tip you have given?
   c   Which employees in a hotel might expect to receive a tip?

2   Read these extracts about tipping taken from guidebooks to Australia, the United States, and the United Kingdom. Complete the chart which follows with details of how much to tip.

Australia

Tipping

Tipping has never been the custom in Australia and many are loath to have it start. Hotels and restaurants do not add service charges but it is a widely accepted practice to tip a waiter 10–12% for good service, although many Australians consider it sufficient to leave only $3 or $4. It is not necessary to tip a hotel doorman for carrying suitcases into the lobby, but porters could be given $1 a bag.

Room Service and housemaids are not tipped except for special service. Taxi drivers do not expect a tip, but you may want to leave any small change. Guides, tour bus drivers, and chauffeurs don't expect tips either, though they are grateful if someone in the group takes up a collection for them. No tipping is necessary in beauty salons or for theater ushers.

Source: Fodor's Australia and New Zealand

USA

UK

Time California and the entire west coast are in the Pacific Standard Time zone, eight hours behind Greenwich Mean Time and three hours behind Eastern Standard Time.

Tipping In restaurants, waiters and waitresses, as well as bartenders, expect a 15% tip; so do taxi drivers and hairdressers. Porters should be tipped 50c to $1 per bag, and parking valets should be given $1. It's nice to leave a few dollars on your pillow for the hotel maid; lavatory attendants will appreciate whatever change you have.

Tourist Offices See 'Information and Money,' earlier in this chapter, as well as specific city chapters later in this guide.

Source: Frommer's California

Tipping

This is as difficult for the locals as it is for visitors. There are no hard and fast rules.

Airport/railway porters: 50p a bag is welcome. There are now red-uniformed Skycaps at airports with a fixed £5 fee.
Hotels: often add a service charge, but porters would expect about 50p a bag going to your room.
Restaurants: almost always include a service charge. Even if the credit card form is left blank next to tips, do not pay again. If not included, a 10% tip is normal, preferably in cash.
Taxis: 10% is normal.
Hairdressers: 10% is normal.

Do not feel obliged to tip unless service has been cheerful and efficient.

Source: Thomas Cook Traveller's London

	USA	UK	Australia
barman	*15%*		
chambermaid			
waiter/waitress			
doorman			
parking valet			
porter			
taxi driver			
tour guide			
lavatory attendant			
hairdresser			
other			

3 In small groups prepare and write a similar paragraph for a guidebook to your country (or a country which you have visited and know well).

11 Vocabulary

48-hour release p. 71, system by which rooms have to be claimed or sold 48 hours (two days) before

allocation p. 71, amount given for a particular purpose (hence **Allocation Holder**)

availability chart p. 71, chart which indicates the number of rooms that can be sold for a particular period

bill p. 67, piece of paper which shows how much money you owe for goods and services; (US) a money note

calculate p. 158 (tapescript), find an answer by using numbers

cash p. 68, money in the form of coins and notes

check out p. 68, pay your bill and leave a hotel

check something through p. 158 (tapescript), examine something written to see if it is correct

cheque p. 68, special piece of paper which you fill in to authorize a bank to pay from your account

comes to p. 67, equals (usually for money amounts)

commission p. 66, money that you get for selling something (usually a percentage)

credit card p. 68, small plastic card that allows you to get goods or services without using money

currency p. 73, money that a particular country uses

deposit p. 69, sum of money which is the first payment for something, with the rest of the money to be paid later

discount p. 71, reduction in the usual price of something (usually a percentage)

exchange rate p. 73, value of the money of one country compared to that of another

expiry date p. 69, end of a period when you can use something

Free Sale Agents p. 71, people or organizations which sell rooms on behalf of a hotel, but without the need to check if rooms are available

imprint p. 69, mark made by pressing an object on a surface (e.g. the writing on a credit card when pressed on paper)

key card p. 158 (tapescript), card given to a guest when they are given their key, when checking in

negotiates p. 71, arranges by discussing with another person or group

receipt p. 68, piece of paper that is given to show you have paid for something

room rate p. 65, fixed amount at which a room in a hotel is charged

sales outlet p. 69, any department in a hotel which sells things to guests (e.g. shop, bar)

service charge p. 68, amount (usually a percentage) added to – for example – a restaurant bill to reward the waiters/waitresses for their work

traveller's cheque p. 68, a cheque that you can change into foreign money when you are travelling abroad

voucher p. 69, a piece of paper exchanged for goods or services

7   Dealing with complaints

1 Speaking

1   In groups, discuss how you would handle the following people complaining in your hotel:

a   A drunk customer in the hotel restaurant complaining loudly about the slow service.

b   A guest who can't speak your language very well, complaining about the size of his/her room (you think).

c   An extremely rude and angry guest complaining about his/her bill when checking out.

d   A dinner guest, who is part of a large and important wedding party, complaining about the quality of the food.

e   An elderly gentleman complaining about how many stairs he has to walk up to get to his room.

f   A foreign visitor to your country complaining about the weather.

Compare your opinions with other groups.

2   Write down three or four similar descriptions of complaints. Pass them to another group to discuss how they would handle them. See if you agree.

2 Reading

1   Before you read the article which follows, discuss this question: How do you think a computer could help to train waiters to cope with people who complain?

2   Read the article and answer the questions which follow.

There's a fly in my software

A computer program trains waiters by simulating restaurant complaints

Does your computer make rude remarks to you? While manufacturers struggle to make their machines more user-friendly, Richard Margetts, a catering lecturer at Granville College, in Yorkshire, has developed a program that positively encourages the computer to be nasty towards its operator.

The software, called Custom, has been funded by the employment department's learning technologies unit, and is designed to help hotel and catering trainees to cope with customers' complaints. Such complaints can make or break a business.

The idea for the program grew out of an unpleasant evening Mr Margetts and his wife had at a hotel. In a scene that could have come from *Fawlty Towers*, the BBC television comedy series, the couple were left standing in the hotel lobby while the receptionist continued making a personal telephone call.

During the meal they were ignored by the waiter and had to order their drinks at the bar and carry them back to the table. The couple complained to the manager who sympathized but said it was difficult to train staff in customer care.

'Britons are very complacent about complaints,' says Mr Margetts, who used to run his own restaurant. 'Good service is not seen as being very important.'

Hence the computer-based training package. The first part analyses how complaints arise. The complaints included those from the few customers who go to a restaurant determined to make a fuss, perhaps in the hope of a free meal.

Mr Margetts says: 'Within the program we have included ways of spotting those complaints, and those that can arise because of a bad experience somebody has had even before entering the restaurant.

'The program will also identify the complaints that can occasionally arise merely from customer boredom. Somebody may have decided he cannot stand his dining companion, for example, and takes his unhappiness out on the food or the unfortunate waiter.'

The waiters assemble a customer profile. 'How am I dressed – shabby, average or immaculate?' the computer asks. 'Is my accent local or non-local? Do I speak perfect English or might I be a tourist? Am I alone or with a group? Is it a mixed-sex group? What is my age bracket? How much alcohol do I seem to have drunk?'

The computer then suggests successful ways of tackling the customer.

Mr Margetts says: 'The idea is that the trainee sees that personal attributes such as accent or dress are a weak indicator of how a customer will respond during a complaint, whereas attitude and alcohol are much stronger.'

In the second part of the program, the computer becomes less than friendly. The trainee takes part in role-play simulations in which the computer acts like a complaining customer.

The computer can be programmed to be angry, rude, reasonable, or rambling. The trainee's task is to recognize the warning signs and calm the situation.

At the end of a session, trainees are told how many attempts it has taken to reach the correct response. The results are saved for the course tutor to read.

But although the program uses graphics and text to good effect, it cannot yet convey complex factors such as the customer's tone of voice, body posture, or facial expression. Future versions may use video pictures and sound for greater realism.

However, Mr Margetts says there are no plans to incorporate a robot arm that grabs the user by the lapels.

GEORGE COLE

Source: The Times

Vocabulary
nasty = unkind
make or break = cause either success or complete failure
make a fuss = cause a lot of problems with no real reason
shabby = dressed in old, untidy clothes
immaculate = perfect, very neat
rambling = talking in a long, unorganized way

a What is Mr Margetts's job?

b Who is the software program going to help?

c What two things did Mr and Mrs Margetts complain about?

d What was the manager's response?

e The article mentions three causes of complaints which are nothing to do with the quality of service or food. What are they?

f What questions does the computer ask in order to construct a customer profile?

g Which factors decide how a customer will react during a complaint?

h During the role play, what must the trainee try to do?

i What does the program *not* do yet?

3 Do you think this form of training is effective? Give reasons.

3 Listening

1 Listen to this conversation between a guest and a receptionist.

  a Make a list of the things the guest is complaining about.
  b What does she want to do?
  c What is the outcome?

2 Now listen to the second conversation. What is the outcome this time?

3 Listen to both conversations again. In what ways does the receptionist behave differently in the second conversation? What does she offer to do?

4 Language study   Present Perfect Passive

Look at these examples from the conversations, where something needed to be done but wasn't:

▶ *The bath **hasn't been cleaned**.*
▶ *The sheets **haven't been changed**.*

1 Match up these nouns and verbs and make similar sentences.

1 bed	4 bin	**a** dust	**d** vacuum
2 carpet	5 shelves	**b** make	**e** empty
3 floor	6 wash-basin	**c** clean	**f** sweep

Example:
The bed hasn't been made.

2 Look at this picture of a hotel at the start of the summer season. It is in very bad condition. Discuss what hasn't been done. Look at the garden, the walls, the paintwork, and so on.

These verbs may help:

cut   mend   repair   fix   replaster   weed   paint   tile

Should have (done)

Look at these examples from the conversation.

▶ *They **should have cleaned** it.*
▶ *You **should have complained** earlier.*

1   Use the same examples that were used in the Present Perfect Passive
    language study to make similar sentences:

Example:
They should have made the bed.

2   Develop each of these statements with a *should have* sentence.

Example:
This room is filthy!
You should have cleaned it.

a   This room is filthy.
b   Why didn't you tell us?
c   Why did that old lady carry her heavy suitcase herself?
d   You're going to be late for work.
e   I didn't know it was going to rain.
f   The hotel turned out to be worse than the one we stayed in last year.
g   I missed the last bus and had to walk home.
h   We've been robbed!

Responding to complaints

Look at this example of responding to a complaint.

Complaint	Apology	Action
▶ *This room is filthy!*	*I'm terribly sorry.*	*I'll send someone up to clean it immediately.*

Now respond to the following complaints in a similar way.

Complaint	Apology	Action
a This soup's disgusting!	_____	_____
b I'm sorry to trouble you, but I don't seem to have any towels.	_____	_____
c It's really noisy. Can't you do something about it?	_____	_____
d The central heating's not working.	_____	_____
e Look. Our sheets haven't been changed.	_____	_____
f Sorry, but I ordered tea, not coffee.	_____	_____
g I can't seem to get the shower to work.	_____	_____

5 Word study

When a speaker wants to emphasize an adjective or make it stronger (especially during an emotional exchange such as complaining and apologizing), it is common to use an *intensifying adverb*, e.g. 'I'm *extremely* sorry.' However, not all combinations of adverb and adjective are possible.

1 Which adjectives can be used with which adverbs? Tick (✓) the appropriate boxes. Some of the combinations were used in the conversations you heard earlier.

	sorry	sure	disappointed	annoyed	unacceptable	filthy
extremely	☐	☐	☐	☐	☐	☐
absolutely	☐	☐	☐	☐	☐	☐
very	☐	☐	☐	☐	☐	☐
terribly	☐	☐	☐	☐	☐	☐
quite	☐	☐	☐	☐	☐	☐

Can you work out any rule?

2 Complete the following sentences with an appropriate adverb/adjective combination from the ones above.

a I'm _____ _____ that I didn't make any international phone calls from my room.

b We were _____ _____ with the hotel, considering that so many people had recommended it to us.

c The standard of the food was terrible. It was _____ _____ .

d The swimming-pool obviously hadn't been cleaned for ages. It was _____ _____ .

e I'm _____ _____ that it's so noisy. Unfortunately, it's unavoidable because we're having essential repairs done.

f The chef is obviously a perfectionist. He gets _____ _____ if the slightest thing goes wrong.

6 Speaking

Divide into pairs, **A** and **B**. Choose one of these areas of complaint (or invent your own):

dirty room   no bathroom
bad/slow service   bed too small
noisy room   rude staff

A

You are the receptionist. You want to calm the guest down. Your tactics are a) to get the guest to say exactly what the problem is; b) to 'buy' time; and c) to offer something that is acceptable and possible.

B

You are the guest. You are extremely angry. Think about a) what exactly is wrong; b) what you expected; and c) what you want to happen.

Now act out the conversation.

7 Reading

1 Look at this advertisement for The Country Village Hotel.

a What facilities does it offer?

b What type of guest would be attracted to the hotel?

The Country Village Hotel

Rural ... Romantic ... Relaxing

❖ Enjoy the peace and quiet of The Country Village Hotel, set in beautiful countryside but only 30 miles from London.

❖ Relax in our luxurious pool, with pool-side bar.

❖ Dine in our romantic restaurant.

❖ A short bus-ride from the delightful town centre of Buckingham.

❖ We'll look after you.

❖ Phone us now for a reservation on 0790 36143.

2   Divide into pairs, **A** and **B**. **A** should read letter 1. **B** should read letter 2. Answer the questions which follow, then compare answers with your partner.

1

Dear Sir,

   I am writing to you concerning my recent stay at your hotel. My wife and I arrived on Saturday 15th May and stayed for a week. Although we were treated well and found the service and your staff excellent, there are one or two matters which we feel we should bring to your attention.

   Firstly, we had hoped for a complete break from our busy work lives, and indeed your advertisement promised 'peace and quiet' and the chance to relax. However, we were surprised to find that there was a lot of noisy building work. I understand that repairs are sometimes needed, but is it really necessary to start at seven o'clock in the morning?

   Secondly, we had hoped to make use of the 'luxurious pool'. To our astonishment, we found that this was closed for the entire period of our stay.

   I hope you do not mind me writing to you about these things, but I would be grateful if you could give me some explanation. As I said at the start, it is a pity when your service is so excellent in other areas.

   I look forward to hearing from you.

Yours faithfully,

Hector Bradley

Mr. Hector Bradley

2

Dear Sir

I recently had the bad luck to stay in your hotel, and I am now forced to write to you to express my disgust with the service you provided.

From the moment I arrived I was treated in an unfriendly manner. I also found that the promises you made in your advertisement were not true. The hotel was not relaxing – it was noisy and uncomfortable. The restaurant was not romantic, and indeed it was hardly a restaurant, as it offered very little variety of food.

Furthermore, there was no transport into town. When I complained about this I was simply told there was a bus strike. Surely you could have provided a taxi service for your guests.

I am a fairly reasonable man, and I am quite prepared to put up with a little inconvenience, but this was too much for me. If I do not receive a satisfactory explanation and appropriate compensation, I shall be forced to take the matter further.

I am sending a copy of this letter to my solicitor and to the local tourist board.

Yours faithfully

P Pryke

P Pryke

a Who is the letter from?
b What is the writer complaining about?
c Was there anything positive?
d What action does the writer want the hotel to take?
e What is the tone of the letter?
f Underline expressions used to complain. Compare them with the spoken expressions in *4 Language study*.

8 Writing

You are the manager of The Country Village Hotel, and you must reply to the unhappy guests. You don't want to make excuses but you know there were reasons why the things promised in the advertisement did not happen. Here are your notes:

PROBLEM	
swimming-pool closed	– essential maintenance due to damage to pump system
incomplete restaurant service	– head chef had to go to hospital suddenly
noisy building work	– building new recreation centre (and this is least busy time of year)
bad transport services	– bus strike

Write a letter to one of the guests apologizing for the difficulties they had, and explaining the reasons. If you want to, you can offer some compensation.

Follow this structure:

Paragraph 1: Thank writer for letter. Make general apology.
Paragraph 2: Make specific apology and give explanation/reasons for each complaint.
Paragraph 3: Offer some compensation (if you want).
Paragraph 4: Repeat general apology and make closing remarks.

Here are some expressions which may be useful:

Thank you for . . .
I was sorry to hear . . .
I would like to explain . . .
I can assure you . . .
As a sign of our concern, we would like to offer . . .
I hope . . .
Please accept . . .

9 Listening

You are going to listen to a woman talking about a disastrous time she had when she stayed in a hotel.

1 Before you listen, think about these questions:

a Have you, or has anyone you know, ever had a disastrous stay in a hotel? What went wrong?

b What could go wrong in these areas?

front desk/checking in
the guest's room
in the restaurant
checking out/the bill

2 Now listen to the woman speaking. What things went wrong during her stay?

3 Listen again. Are these statements true (T) or false (F)?

a ☐ The woman had seen an advertisement for the hotel in a shop window.
b ☐ The couple went to the hotel to celebrate a birthday.
c ☐ The man at the front desk had probably been arguing.
d ☐ They were given the key to room 106.
e ☐ The woman complained about the size of the bathroom.
f ☐ They didn't complain in the restaurant.
g ☐ They didn't sleep very well because they heard a screaming noise.
h ☐ They quite enjoyed the breakfast.
i ☐ They went to another hotel after checking out.
j ☐ The murder took place in room 107.

10 Activity

1 Divide into two groups, **A** and **B**. In your groups, prepare for the role play by reading your instructions. Group **A**, your instructions are on page 143. Group **B**, your instructions are on page 148.

2 Feedback discussion:

  a How well did the waiters cope with the pressure?

  b Can you work out any general strategies for dealing with 'difficult' guests?

  c Has the experience changed your ideas about a waiter's job in any way?

11 Activity

1 Read the summary of answers to a hotel feedback questionnaire:

  a Do you think the manager will be pleased with the results?

  b In which areas of the hotel service were the results most disappointing?

2 In small groups, discuss what can be done to improve the hotel service.

  a What changes can be made?

  b How will you approach the different members of staff involved?

Compare your opinions with other groups.

A Question of Service
(All figures are %)

	Yes	No	Not applicable
1 If you stayed between Monday and Friday, were you met by the Hotel Lobby Manager?	5	70	25
2 Did the Lobby Manager explain the facilities and services that the hotel had to offer?	2	73	25
3 Were you asked about your check-out requirements when you booked in?	60	40	0
4 Did you feel that you received a warm welcome to the hotel?	20	80	0
5 If you received a message while you were in the hotel, did you receive it within 10 minutes of being able to receive it?	15	5	80
6 Were you addressed by name in the reception/lobby?	2	98	0
7 Were you addressed by name in the restaurant?	10	90	0
8 If you received a morning call, was it on time?	70	0	30
9 Were you addressed by name when receiving your morning call?	65	5	30
10 Were you offered a choice of smoking or non-smoking table in our restaurant?	55	30	15
11 Were you offered a choice of smoking or non-smoking bedroom?	83	17	0

	Yes	No	Not applicable
12 If you asked for the one-number room-service facility, did it operate to your satisfaction?	55	5	40
13 If you took breakfast during your stay, were you met on arrival in the restaurant and shown to your seat?	21	59	20
14 Did you receive your breakfast within your time expectations?	5	75	20
15 Was table service available in the lounge bar?	35	35	30

	Excellent	Good	Fair	Unacceptable
16 Reception and Lobby	0	15	65	20
17 Bars	35	40	25	0
18 Restaurant – quality of service	20	63	12	5
19 Lunch/Dinner – quality of food	50	35	12	3
20 Breakfast – quality of food	5	15	71	9
21 Bedrooms	33	47	20	0

22 In general, having experienced the facilities of this stay, would you choose to stay in this hotel again?	55 **Yes**	45 **No**
23 As a result of the service and hospitality that you have received, would you choose to stay in this hotel again?	42 **Yes**	58 **No**

12 Vocabulary

annoyed p. 82, fairly angry

apology p. 81, statement to say that you are sorry for something

appalling p. 161 (tapescript), shocking or terrible

arguing p. 86, saying things (often angrily) to show that you do not agree with somebody

calm or **calm down** p. 78, become or make somebody become quiet when they are angry or upset

complain p. 85, say that you are not satisfied or happy with something, *n* **complaint** p. 78

complimentary p. 160 (tapescript), given free of charge

cope with p. 78, deal successfully with

disastrous p. 86, very bad or harmful

disgusting p. 81, causing a strong feeling of dislike

dust p. 80, remove small pieces of dirt from shelves and surfaces with a cloth

empty p. 80, remove the contents of something (e.g. ashtray, waste-paper bin)

filthy p. 81, very dirty

ignored p. 78, paid no attention to

lapels p. 78, the two parts of the front of a jacket that are folded back

lobby p. 87, entrance-hall

make excuses p. 85, give reasons (true or untrue) in order to explain a mistake or bad behaviour

overcooked p. 161 (tapescript), cooked too much

repair p. 80, put something old or damaged back into good condition; mend

replaster p. 80, repair walls by covering them with a special mixture of sand, lime and water to make them smooth

rural p. 83, of or in the countryside

session p. 78, period spent doing one particular thing

sweep p. 80, clean by removing dirt or dust with a brush

sympathized p. 78, understood and shared somebody's feelings

tasteless p. 161 (tapescript), having no taste or flavour

threatened to p. 161 (tapescript), warned that

tile p. 80, put tiles (thin pieces of baked clay used as a roof covering) on a roof

trainees p. 78, people being trained for a job

unacceptable p. 82, not good enough

vacuum p. 80, clean (a carpet) with a special machine

weed p. 80, remove the unwanted plants from a garden

8 Off-site services

1 Reading

Hotels arrange off-site services for guests. These may be excursions, walking tours, sporting activities, and so on. What excursions and extra events do you think these hotels will offer?

1 Sheraton Towers City Hotel, San Francisco
2 Arina Sands Beach Hotel, Crete
3 Greenacres Country Hotel, England

Look at the excursions and extra events below, and decide which ones would be offered at each of the three hotels.

a Plane trip over the Grand Canyon.
b Drinking, dining, and dancing! Greek village night.
c Come on a romantic evening Bay cruise to the Golden Gate.
d If you like sea and sun, you'll love our cruise to Santorini.
e Trip to wine country.
f Enjoy the countryside: hire a bicycle.
g Agricultural Museum and Park – special discount tickets available.
h Thirsty? Then what about coming on the pub evening?
i Car hire. Excellent rates.
j Feeling adventurous? Why don't you try water-skiing?
k Experience the outdoor beauty from horseback. Come pony-trekking.
l Visit the archaeological site of Knossos: the earliest civilization.
m Tour of the caves by boat.
n Bring the kids to the Cable Car Museum: they'll love it!
o Do you want to come hill-walking?
p All-day deep-sea fishing trip. Why not catch your own supper?

2 Listening

1 Look at the excursion booking form for the Arina Sands Hotel:

   a What do the abbreviations Dr and Pax stand for?

   b How much does it cost for two adults and one child to go on the 'Cultural Crete' excursion and the 'Who pays the ferryman?' excursion? Don't forget to include entrance fees.

   c Can guests pay in dollars?

Thomson Holidays *Excursion booking form*

Name: _____   Hotel: _____   Room No: _____

Day	Excursion	* NB		Price in Dr	Pax	Total
a ____	Cultural Crete	* 1	Adult Child	5100 2550		
Tuesday	Countryside	* 2	Adult Child	4100 2050		
Tuesday	Best of the **b**____		Adult Child	**c**____ 3200		
Wednesday	Knossos	* 3	Adult Child	3900 1950		
Wednesday	Raki & Syrtaki evening		Adult Child	**d**____ 4550		
Thursday	Who pays the ferryman?	* 4	Adult Child	5800 2900		
Friday	Eastern Explorer		Adult Child	6400 3200		
e____	Knossos	* 3	Adult Child	3900 1950		
Saturday	Who pays the ferryman?	* 4	Adult Child	5800 2900		
f____	Samaria Adventure	* 5	Adult Child	6700 3350		
Sunday	Samaria Glimpses	* 6	Adult Child	5900 2950		
Mon, Wed, Thu, **g**____	Santorini **h**____	* 7	Adult Child	11000 5500		

* All entrance fees are extra

* 1- 400DR   church   * 4- 400DR   entrance
     800DR   Phaestos   * 5- 855DR   boat
     400DR   Gortys   500DR   entrance
* 2- 400DR   cave   * 6- 1600DR boat
     400DR   Monastery   500DR   entrance
* 3 -1000DR entrance   * 7- 800DR   transfer to port
     1000DR   museum

Please make your bookings at the welcome party to avoid disappointment, as places cannot be guaranteed afterwards.

■ Payment is accepted in drachmas only.
■ All coaches are fully insured and air-conditioned.
■ All excursions are guided by a professional guide or company representative.
■ Cancellation fees will be incurred if less than 24 hours' notice is given.

---

2 You are going to listen to a representative at the hotel talking to guests about the excursions they can take. As you listen, complete the missing information on the Excursion Booking Form.

3 Listen again and note the details of these three tours:

a Knossos

b Raki and Syrtaki evening

c Samaria adventure

3 Language study First Conditional

In the talk, a number of First Conditional sentences were used. Look at these examples.

If + Present Tense, will

▶ *If you come on the tour, **you'll see** a fine example of Minoan civilization.*

▶ *If you are fit and like adventure, **you'll love** this trip.*

If + Present Tense, modal verb

▶ *If you have any questions, **you can** ask me when I come round.*

If + Present Tense, Imperative

▶ *If you come, **bring** plenty of water.*

Note: the 'result' clause can come first.

Example:
What will we do if it rains? or *If it rains, what will we do?*

1 Expand these sentences about the excursion to Santorini:

a If/go/Santorini/see/volcanic island

b If/go/Santorini cruise/return/midnight?

c Have/donkey ride/if/go/Santorini

d If/sunbathe/not forget/sun-cream

2 Use the notes you made about the other excursions to make similar sentences.

Giving advice

Look at the ways the representative gave advice:

▶ ***Why don't you*** *come on the Cultural Crete excursion?*
▶ ***If I were you,*** *I'd wait till the Thursday or Friday.*
▶ ***You could always*** *spend a day or two exploring the town here.*

1 Can you think of other ways of giving advice?

2 Now give advice to the person making the statements below:

   a I've lost my passport.
   b I've got a terrible headache.
   c I can't find my keys.
   d We'd like to eat some traditional local food.
   e What should I visit while I'm staying here?
   f What's a good present to take home?
   g Which wine do you recommend with the chicken?
   h I can't think where to go for my next holiday.

4 Speaking   Look at this description of Charleston in the USA:

Charleston, on the coast of South Carolina, is one of America's most historic towns. It was rice and indigo which first made it rich. Nowadays it contains many beautiful historic houses and museums as well as interesting shops and restaurants. The Old Town is fascinating to walk around, or you can take one of the guided coach or horse-and-carriage tours. There is also plenty to see in the surrounding area.

Fort Sumter & Harbor Tours
Only Customers With Tickets Allowed on Pier

Divide into pairs, **A** and **B**. **A**, your instructions are on page 144. **B**, your instructions are on page 148.

5 Word study

1 Complete these pairs of events and places of entertainment.

	Event	Place
a	play	theatre
b	concert	_____
c	_____	stadium
d	disco	_____
e	exhibition	_____
f	musical	_____
g	_____	cinema

Find out which of these events the rest of the class like going to in their free time.

2 Look at this list of facilities offered on a coach tour. Fill in the gaps with one of the words underneath.

a _____ from your hotel

b _____ at your hotel

c expert and _____ guide

d _____ charges included in price

e lunch _____ in price

f modern coach with _____ or heating

g _____ seats

h no _____ charge

i _____ on the coach

j _____ in own language

k tea and coffee _____ on the coach

air-conditioning	drop-off	pick-up
available	entertaining	reclining
cancellation	entrance	toilets
commentary	included	

6 Reading

Car hire is another service which many hotels provide.

1 Discuss these questions with a partner:

a What things should you look for or check when you hire a car?
b What type of things can go wrong?

2 Read the information sheet about hiring a car from Hertz, and match these headings with the relevant paragraphs.

What's included
Drive away with ease
Delivery free to your door
If you book with Hertz . . .
Availability guaranteed
Excellent value for money
The highest standards of service

iii) delivered FREE to your doorstep
and all at a great value price that's hard to beat.

b _____

Your car will usually be no more than seven months old, or will have covered no more than 31,000 (50,000 kms) AND will have passed a 19-point delivery check on all important mechanical and other parts prior to rental. Furthermore, all cars will be delivered to you thoroughly cleaned, both inside and out.

c _____

To help you make the most of your holiday motoring, Hertz will give you an area road map. Parents can rest assured that all four-door cars are equipped with rear-door child-proof locks and that child safety seats are normally available at a small additional charge.

a _____

You'll enjoy the reliability of a car that's:
i) usually a maximum of seven months old
ii) checked, cleaned, and with full tank of petrol

d _____

Not only are the prices very competitive, but they are inclusive of:

i)   delivery and collection
ii) unlimited mileage
iii) 3rd party, fire and theft insurance
iv) collision damage waiver, which covers the renter's responsibility for accidental damage to the vehicle
v)   all local taxes

e _____

Your car will be delivered to your hotel or apartment free of charge with a full tank of petrol and collected from you again at the end of the rental. Should you experience any difficulty with the car, a replacement vehicle, if necessary, will be delivered to you as quickly as possible.

f _____

When you pre-book your Hertz car, availability is guaranteed, provided that you indicate your requirement at the time of booking your holiday.

g _____

i)   Delivery and collection to and from your hotel or apartment.
ii) Unlimited mileage.
iii) Insurance cover for: third party, fire and theft, Bail Bond in Spain, the Balearics and the Canary Islands, but exclusive of Personal Accident (see below) and contents cover.
iv) Expenditure on oil and maintenance repairs, which will be refunded on production of receipts at the end of the rental.
v)   Local government taxes.
vi) Collision damage waiver, which covers renter's responsibility for damage to the vehicle.

Source: Thomson Summer Sun brochure

3 Are these statements true (T) or false (F)?

a ☐ Cars are never more than seven months old.
b ☐ You have to collect the car from a garage.
c ☐ When you get the car it will not be dirty.
d ☐ You do not need to buy a local road map.
e ☐ You must pay local taxes.
f ☐ If you have a problem with the car it will be changed.
g ☐ You can drive as far as you want without paying extra.
h ☐ You must pay for any oil and maintenance repairs you need.

7 Speaking

Divide into pairs, **A** and **B**. **A** is the representative of a car hire company working at a hotel desk. **B** is a hotel guest. When you have prepared your roles, act out the conversation.

A
Ask the guest about the following things: How long for? When? Licence? Type of car? Method of payment? Be prepared to answer any questions the guest may have.

B
Think about the following things: How long for? When from? How many people? Type of car? Find out exactly what is included in the price and what isn't.

8 Listening   Listen to this guided tour of Charleston.

1   As you listen, put these attractions into the order in which they are
    mentioned by the guide.

a ☐	St Michael's Church	f ☐	Ashley River Memorial Bridge
b ☐	Calhoun Mansion	g ☐	Gibbes Museum of Art
c ☐	The Old Market	h ☐	Charles Towne Landing
d ☐	King Street	i ☐	USS Yorktown
e ☐	Battery/White Point Gardens	j ☐	Heyward-Washington House

Can you identify the points on the map?

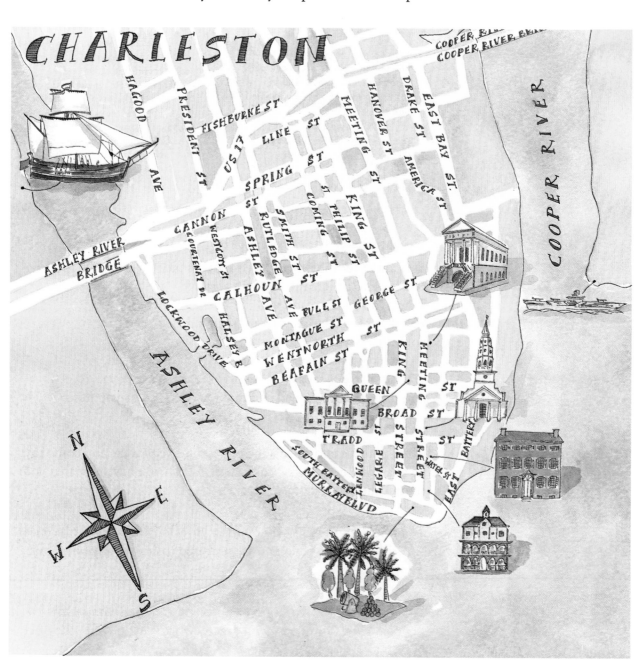

2 Listen again and indicate whether these statements are true (T) or false (F).

a ☐ The driver's name is Tom.
b ☐ The air-conditioning needs to be adjusted.
c ☐ St Michael's Church was built in 1671.
d ☐ One of the historic houses was built by George Washington.
e ☐ The Battery is also known as White Point Gardens.
f ☐ The tour arrives at the Calhoun Mansion at 4 p.m.
g ☐ The Charles Towne Landing is on the other side of the river.
h ☐ At the end, the guide takes the group shopping.

9 Activity

You are going to read about the Evan Evans full-day coach tour to Leeds Castle, Canterbury, and Dover. Divide into pairs, **A**, and **B**. **A**, your text is on page 145. **B**, your text is on page 149. When you have read your text, write the questions you must ask to find out the missing information from your partner. Then ask your partner the questions and fill in the gaps in your leaflet. At the end, you can check your answers by looking at your partner's leaflet.

10 Activity

Choose an area you know well – for example, your home town.

Make a list of the attractions and local facilities which might interest a visitor. Make notes about each of the places you have listed.

Draw a rough map of the area and decide on the best route for a tour (either walking or by coach).

Divide into groups of three or four (if possible, each member of the group should have chosen a different place).

Imagine you are a guide leading a group of visitors (the others in your group). Take them on a 'guided tour' of your map telling them about the places they are seeing. 'Visitors' can ask questions if they want.

11 Writing

Write a leaflet describing the attractions and facilities of the area you made notes about in *10 Activity* . The leaflet is for inclusion in the 'Welcome Information' pack of a hotel.

Include information on:
attractions and sights
sightseeing tours
entertainment and shopping

Look at these examples taken from a leaflet about Charleston to help you.

Gibbes Museum of Art

One of the finest collections of American art in the South-East. The collection consists of views of Charleston, portraits of notable South Carolinians, paintings, prints, and drawings from the 18th century to the present. The Museum Shop features an outstanding selection of fine art prints, posters, cards, jewelry, and books. Tues.-Sat. 10-5, Sun. & Mon. 1-5. Closed holidays. Adults $3; senior citizens (ages 62 and older), military, and college students (with ID cards) $2: children ages 6-18 $1; children under 6 free with adult. 135 Meeting St., Charleston, SC 29401. (803) 722-2706. See ad page 11. Map location 51-S.

The Old Exchange & Provost Dungeon

Over 300 years of pirates, presidents, patriots, and preservation make the Old Exchange and Provost Dungeon one of the most historic places you'll see on your visit to Charleston. Built by the British in 1771, it was Charleston's first customs house and exchange, and the former site of a British colonial jail. The self-guided tour highlights the dungeon where British officers imprisoned American patriots, the Great Hall where George Washington was lavishly entertained in 1791, and the original trading floor of the Exchange. Don't forget to visit our gift shop. Open daily 9-5. Admission. 122 East Bay St. at Broad St. (803) 727-2165. See ad page 3. Map location 52-V.

Gray Line Tours

Explore America's most historic city with the world's most experienced sight-seeing company. Historic Charleston tours leave several times daily with pick-ups at downtown hotels and the visitor center. These tours cover large areas of the peninsula city, including all major landmarks, with narration by professional guides, and our comfortable vehicles are customized for Charleston's narrow streets. Visit to historic house included in most tours. Seasonal tours to plantations and gardens. For reservations on all tours call 722-4444 or see driver at the Visitor Reception Center, map location 42-R. See coupon page 11.

Talk of the Towne

Let a quality owner-operated tour service show you the Battery, the Market, the College of Charleston, and much more! 1-hour plus tours offer a comprehensive sightseeing experience that covers more than 6 miles: 2-hour tours also include a guided historic house tour. THE ONLY TOUR THAT VISITS THE NATHANIEL RUSSELL HOUSE is offered twice daily. Tours depart from the Visitor Reception Center, map location 42-R, with free downtown hotel pick-ups. For reservations and information call 795-8199. See coupon page 23.

12 Vocabulary

admission p. 144, the money charged for entering a place open to the public (also **entrance fees** p. 90, or **entrance charge** p. 93)

adventurous p. 89, liking excitement and liking to try new things

archaeological site p. 89, place where ancient buildings have been dug up

attractions p. 98, places which are worth seeing in a town or resort

cancellation fee or **charge** p. 93, the money which a customer must pay if they decide not to take a service which they have booked

child-proof p. 94, which cannot be operated by children

collision damage waiver (CDW) p. 94, special insurance which means you do not have to pay anything if your hire car is damaged in an accident

commentary p. 93, spoken description of something as it happens (e.g. tour)

cruise p. 89, holiday or tour travelling by boat and visiting a number of different places

drop-off p. 93, place where people can get off a coach

entertainment p. 98, things to do that interest and amuse people

equipped with p. 94, provided with the things necessary to do something

excursion p. 90, short journey made for pleasure (usually a group of people)

exhibition p. 93, collection of things shown publicly

for inclusion p. 98, to be included

fort p. 144, strong building used for military defence

guaranteed p. 90, promised with certainty

hire p. 89, have the use of something for a short time by paying for it

included p. 93, part of the price; see also **inclusive of** p. 94

mileage p. 94, distance travelled (measured in miles)

pax p. 90, abbreviation for 'passengers'

pick-up p. 93, place where passengers can get on a coach

play p. 93, dramatic performance, usually in a theatre

reclining p. 93, that can be adjusted so that you can lie back

ruins p. 162 (tapescript), buildings that have been badly damaged

sightseeing p. 98, visiting the famous places in a city as a tourist

stadium p. 93, building where sporting events take place

surrounding p. 92, which is around or nearby

theatre p. 93, building where plays and other shows are performed

third party, fire and theft p. 94, special insurance covering particular damage and loss to a car

vacation p. 163 (tapescript), holiday (especially in US)

9 The business traveller

1 Listening

Hotels like to make sure their important guests enjoy a superior service. You are going to listen to a Front Office Manager explain how his hotel treats its important guests differently.

1 Before you listen, consider:
   a What kind of business guests are important for a hotel?
   b What can a hotel do before and on the arrival of an important guest to make their stay comfortable and easy?

2 Listen to the Front Office Manager explain his hotel's policy and complete the table below.

Class of Guest	Typical Job/Position	Before Arrival	On Arrival
VIP (very important person)			
CIP (company important person)			
VVP (very very important person)			

2 Word study

Notice how we make comparisons between things:

▶ *Like any other company, we need to be able to identify important customers.*

Like is followed by a noun, e.g. company.

▶ *Just as an airline will offer a better quality service to first-class passengers, we will provide a higher standard for our important guests.*

Just as is followed by a subject and verb, e.g. an airline will offer . . .

Notice how we make contrasts between things:

▶ *Unlike the normal business guest, the VIP has his or her room allocated in advance.*

Unlike is followed by a noun, e.g. guest.

▶ *Whereas CIP rooms are double-checked, all VVP rooms are treble-checked.*

Whereas is followed by a subject and verb, e.g. CIP rooms are . . .

Complete the sentences below with the appropriate word or words:

a Many Americans like to have tea and toast for breakfast, _____ most British do.

b _____ letters, faxes are a means of immediate communication.

c _____ the venue for this year's conference is Vancouver, next year we'll be in Hawaii.

d _____ charge cards, credit cards are a common means of paying hotel bills.

e _____ economy class, business class can be quite expensive.

f _____ the location of a hotel is important for tourists, it is crucial for business travellers, too.

g _____ this year business is looking up, last year was disastrous.

h _____ VIPs, CIPs get special treatment at most hotels.

i _____ hostels, hotels offer en suite rooms, as well as many additional facilities.

j He earns £8,000 a year, _____ she earns at least £25,000 including bonuses.

3 Language study   Present Perfect Continuous vs Present Perfect Simple

Notice how we use the Present Perfect Continuous:

▶ *Some of our guests* **have been coming** *here for years.*
▶ *He's (has)* **been writing** *a report since three o'clock.*

We use the Present Perfect Continuous with a phrase saying *how long*.

Compare this with the Present Perfect Simple:

▶ *We've* **had** *lots of VIPs here this week.*
▶ *He's (has)* **written** *twenty pages of his report.*

We use the Present Perfect Simple with a phrase saying *how many* or *how much*.

Put the verbs in the following sentences into the correct form:

a I (save)_____ for two years. I (save)_____ £1,000.

b Since lunch-time, Mary (read)_____ the newspaper. She (read)_____ half of it.

c I (only play)_____ a few games of squash because I (only play)_____ it for a while.

d I (drink)_____ coffee all day. I (drink)_____ eight cups.

e (you only read)_____ the first chapter? You (read)_____ that book for ages.

f Albert (not work)_____ there for long, but he (already be promoted)_____ twice.

g I (sit)_____ at my typewriter since eight o'clock this morning, but I (only manage)_____ to write four letters.

h Belinda (play)_____ tennis since she was five, and it shows – she (win)_____ every competition she's entered in the last two years.

4 Reading   **1** What special facilities do business travellers expect? Make a list.

2 Read the text about the Copthorne Tara Business Apartments. In what ways are the facilities they offer similar to or different from the list you have made?

*W*hen you are away on business, you need a place which is equipped for and conducive to business. Somewhere quite unlike the average hotel room. But you need to know you'll have a comfortable stay, too.

With this in mind, the **Copthorne Tara Hotel** now offers the unique Business Apartment: a high-quality bedroom linked to a fully-equipped office meeting room for up to six people, with its own separate cloak-room/toilet facilities.

The perfect setting

The Copthorne Tara has a particular understanding of the needs of the busy executive, and each Business Apartment is furnished to create the professional atmosphere in which you would wish to do business.

The bedrooms, separate but intercon-necting with the office meeting rooms, are of the Copthorne Tara's usual high standard, with private bathroom, TV, and telephone.

The right facilities

The equipment in your Business Apartment has been carefully chosen to place at your fingertips all the essentials of the modern office: fax/copier, phones, and PC with printer (loaded with the latest Lotus and WordPerfect software).

A VHS player and teletext television are conveniently situated for group viewing. A screen is ceiling-mounted for use with slide or overhead projector (available on request) and there is a large white marker board, a flip-chart, and supply of stationery.

Fridge and tea- and coffee-making facilities are provided, and full room service is, of course, available at all times.

---

5 Listening

Listen to this interview with Margaret Sesnan, a business executive who travels a lot in her job.

1   Before you listen, match these words with their definitions:

1 exhibition	**a** soft shoes worn only at home
2 slippers	**b** a very large show of goods, advertising, etc., for people who work in a particular industry
3 stand (noun)	**c** an area or structure where things are displayed, exhibited, or sold
4 trade fair	**d** a show for the public

2 Now answer these questions:

 a What is Margaret's job and what type of business trips does she go on?
 b How are the trips arranged?
 c What business facilities does she look for in a hotel?
 d What special features does she look for as a woman?
 e What different customs does she mention at business appointments in Japan?

3 Margaret said that she prefers to be on a lower floor and near the lift for safety reasons.

Working in pairs, discuss what other special needs you think travelling female business executives have. Consider facilities and security features.

6 Speaking

Business nowadays is very much an international and multinational activity. It is often in the hotel where the cultural differences resulting from this fact are most evident.

1 What special cultural difficulties and needs would an American business person have in your country?

Think about social customs/behaviour, greeting people and meeting in general, language difficulties, food and eating habits (and meal table etiquette), and business situations (dress, negotiating, making deals, etc.).

2 How would a hotel find out about the details of these different cultural practices and customs?

3 What can the hotel do to help people of different nationalities and cultures feel at home and feel able to mix with others?

Think about reception procedures, room design and facilities, information sheets and signs, restaurants, and staffing.

7 Reading

A significant proportion of business travellers are Japanese, and some hotels try to cater for their specific requirements.

1 Before you read the text, think about these questions:

 a Why would a Japanese visitor probably not want to stay in room 444?
 b What particular features would a Japanese visitor want to find in a hotel bathroom?
 c Would a Japanese couple prefer twin beds or a double bed?

2   Now read the article to check your answers.

How hoteliers can prepare to welcome their Japanese visitors

The following points suggest how hoteliers can make adjustments to satisfy Japanese visitors' requirements.

The manager or a senior member of staff should be on duty when a party of Japanese visitors is checking in and should preferably have a Japanese business card and a lapel badge. This person should, if possible, remain as their main contact in the hotel throughout their stay and extend a personal welcome and farewell. To say goodbye is extremely important in Japan.

Avoid putting Japanese visitors in rooms with the number 4, 44, 444, etc., as this is considered unlucky. Four is 'Shi' in Japanese, the verb 'to die' being 'Shinu', so this superstition should be taken seriously. Some hotels in Asia do not designate a 4th floor at all.

Ensure a consistently prompt response for service, as well as complaints, in all departments. The Japanese are used to abundant staff on duty and a high level of service. This may initially require a higher level of staffing, but the benefits in terms of future business are obvious.

A welcome sign in Japanese at the reception desk is much appreciated. Exit and other directional signs in Japanese throughout the hotel will make the guests feel more at home.

Try to have at least one Japanese national on your staff; the other staff should receive basic training in Japanese language and should receive cross-cultural training.

Japanese print should be available at Reception or in rooms, for example, a letter of welcome and guidance notes, general information,

Yellow Pages, a city guide, and a newspaper. Sources of Japanese publications could also be provided.

A selection of toiletries and a hair-drier should be provided in bathrooms. It is also appreciated if a yukata (cotton dressing-gown) and slippers are provided in rooms.

Bathrooms must have a constant supply of hot water and should have a bath and shower attachment. The Japanese are accustomed at home to showering outside the bath tub before soaking in a tub of clean water. There should be a drain in the bathroom floor, or else a notice in Japanese and at least one other language, advising on the correct use of the shower and bath. This could prevent flooding or other damage caused through misunderstanding.

Twin beds should be provided for Japanese guests rather than double beds, even for honeymooners.

In the case of groups, care should be taken to give all members rooms of a similar standard.

For refreshment, the Japanese like to have green tea bags, plum tea sachets, and miso soup packets in their rooms with kettle, cups, and saucers.

The Japanese like to see evidence of a high level of security, especially with so many ladies travelling unaccompanied. Relevant information could be provided in room literature and promotional leaflets.

For the business visitor, some hotels provide a Business Centre staffed with Japanese linguists, offering translation and word processing services.

Source: Britain Welcomes Japan prospectus, British Tourist Authority

3   According to the text, which of these things are especially important to a Japanese visitor?

a plenty of staff on duty	**e** politeness
b notices and signs in Japanese	**f** a high level of security
c TV and video in their room	**g** Japanese newspapers
d a Japanese-speaking staff member	**h** Japanese food

8 Writing

Imagine you are the representative of a group of Americans coming to stay in a hotel in your country. Look back at your notes from *6 Speaking* and write a Welcome Letter for the group.

9 Activity

In this activity you are going to design a business apartment. Using the outline plan of a business apartment at the Copthorne Tara Hotel, decide where you would put the items below.

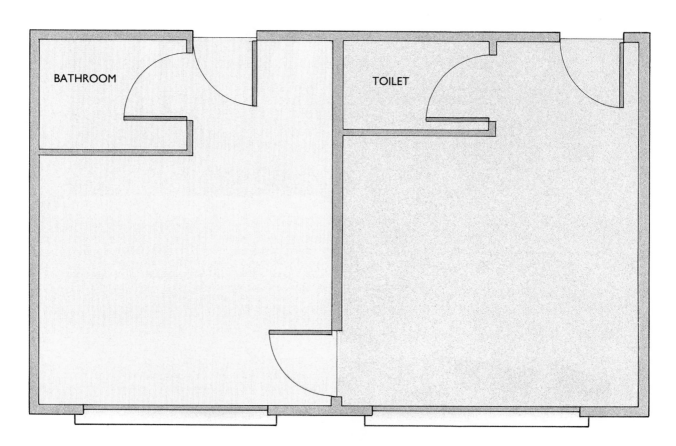

dressing-table   phones and fax
double bed   wardrobe
whiteboard   armchair
screen   flip-chart
coffee-table   bedside table
TV and video   cupboard
overhead projector   meeting table and chairs
slide projector   PC and printer
sink

Compare your design with the true version on page 108.

10 Activity

The following table is taken from comprehensive surveys conducted by American Express covering over 2,000 large and medium-sized companies across all major business sectors during 1989, 1990, and 1991. The four countries involved were the UK, Germany, France, and Switzerland. In each country, the research covered at least 400 companies.

Look at the table below and read the sentences to discover which country is A, which one is B, etc.

Hotels – who's entitled to what?

	A	B	C	D
Directors				
Luxury/4-Star	33%	74%	87%	79%
3-Star	37%	8%	9%	3%
2-Star	11%	5%	—	—
Depends	19%	13%	4%	18%
Senior Managers				
Luxury/4-Star	18%	59%	71%	64%
3-Star	55%	19%	21%	18%
2-Star	15%	5%	2%	—
Depends	12%	17%	6%	18%
Sales/Field Force				
Luxury/4-Star	3%	34%	28%	19%
3-Star	23%	24%	44%	31%
2-Star	43%	13%	7%	15%
Depends	31%	29%	21%	35%

a In Germany, most directors were allowed to stay in luxury/four-star hotels.

b In Switzerland, more of the sales/field force stayed in three-star accommodation than in luxury hotels.

c In France and Switzerland, some senior managers were restricted to two-star accommodation.

d In Switzerland, very few directors used three-star hotels.

e Some German directors stayed in two-star hotels.

f A smaller percentage of UK senior managers were obliged to use three-star hotels than their Swiss counterparts.

11 Vocabulary

abundant p. 105, more than enough

access to p. 165 (tapescript), chance to use

additional extras p. 164 (tapescript), things which are given but are not normally included

at your fingertips p. 103, very near you, ready for use

cloakroom p. 103, room where visitors can leave their coats, bags, etc.

conducive to p. 103, helpful for

counterparts p. 107, people in a similar position

cross-cultural training p. 105, training which helps people to understand different cultures

crucial p. 101, very important

designate p. 105, give a name or number to

distinguish between p. 164 (tapescript), show the difference between

double-checked p. 101, checked twice

dressing-gown p. 105, loose coat worn indoors, usually before dressing

duty manager p. 164 (tapescript), the most senior manager working in the front office at any given time

farewell p. 105, goodbye

flip-chart p. 103, large pad of paper on a board, used when giving presentations, etc.

flooding p. 105, covering the floor with water

honeymooners p. 105, people who have just got married

interconnecting with p. 103, joined to

kettle p. 105, container for boiling water

linguists p. 105, people who know about or who can speak languages well

loaded with sth p. 103, with sth in its memory

off my own bat p. 165 (tapescript), without being told to do it

prompt p. 105, fast, without delay

restricted to p. 107, only allowed to use

sachets p. 105, sealed plastic or paper packs containing a small amount of a product

sales/field force p. 107, people who sell a company's products

screen p. 103, blank surface onto which pictures are projected

soaking p. 105, relaxing in the bath for a long time

stationery p. 103, paper, pens, envelopes, etc.

status p. 164 (tapescript), social or professional position

superstition p. 105, belief for which there is no good reason

teletext p. 103, service which provides news and information in written form on television

the vast majority of p. 107, most

top of the range p. 164 (tapescript), the best of them all

treble-checked p. 101, checked three times

unaccompanied p. 105, alone, without a companion

venue p. 101, place where people meet for a large event, for example a sports contest, a concert or a conference

VHS p. 103, video recording system

were obliged to p. 107, had to

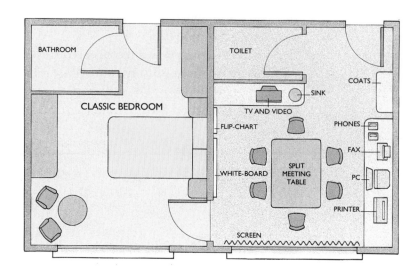

Mr Wrightson
Conference & Banqueting Manager
Grosvenor House Hotel
Park Lane
LONDON W1

6th January 199—

Dear Mr Wrightson

I am writing to you regarding a conference we are
planning to hold in October of this year.

We are looking for a venue in central London and
we anticipate approximately fifty delegates who
will stay for two nights, probably on a Friday and
a Saturday. We will require a large banqueting
room for opening and closing events and a number
of smaller meeting rooms for other sessions.
We will also need to mount an exhibition.

I would be grateful if you could send me some
information about your conference facilities
together with your current rates, and any
information you may have on social events which
can be arranged to accompany the conference.
I would welcome the opportunity
of discussing possible
arrangements with you.

Yours sincerely

B. White

Brenda White
Conference Co-ordinator
ETOA

1 Reading

Read this letter from the Conference Co-ordinator of the European Tour
Operators Association (ETOA).

1 As you read, answer these questions:

   a When is the conference planned for?
   b How many people will be coming?
   c What information does the Conference Co-ordinator want?

2 What type of meetings and events (business and social) do you think a
conference of European tour operators will want? What facilities and
equipment will they require?

2 Word study

1 Can you identify these items of conference equipment? Match these words to the pictures.

a Autocue   **c** overhead projector (OHP)   **e** lectern
b video recorder   **d** public address (PA) system

2 Look at these plans of seating arrangements. What type of meeting are they suitable for? Choose from the list which follows. Make a different design if you think it is more suitable for any of the meetings.

1 lecture   **4** product launch   **7** workshop   **10** formal dinner
2 wedding meal   **5** board meeting   **8** press conference
3 speech   **6** seminar   **9** signing ceremony

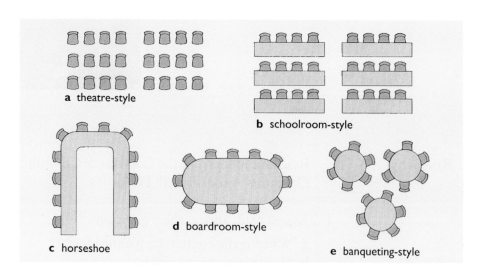

3 Listening

Listen to this conversation between the Conference and Banqueting Manager of the Grosvenor House Hotel in London, and the Conference Co-ordinator of the ETOA. They are discussing the Albemarle Suite.

As you listen, label the names of the rooms and complete the information about size and equipment.

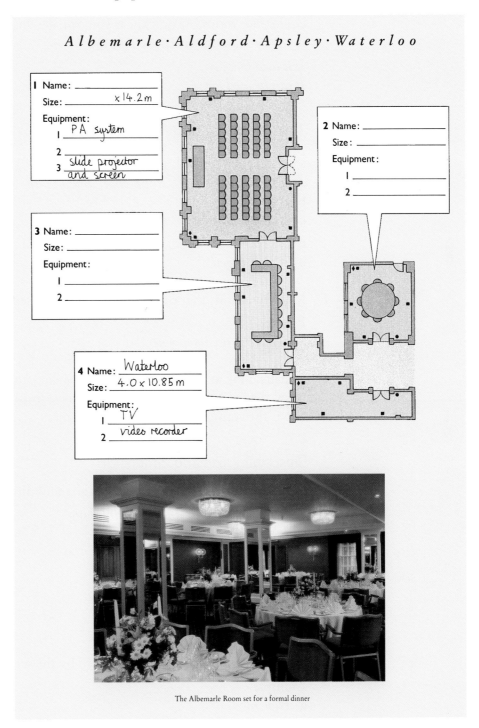

A l b e m a r l e · A l d f o r d · A p s l e y · W a t e r l o o

1 Name: _____
Size: _____ x 14.2 m
Equipment:
1 _____ PA system _____
2 _____
3 _____ slide projector and screen _____

2 Name: _____
Size: _____
Equipment:
1 _____
2 _____

3 Name: _____
Size: _____
Equipment:
1 _____
2 _____

4 Name: _____ Waterloo _____
Size: _____ 4.0 x 10.85 m _____
Equipment:
1 _____ TV _____
2 _____ video recorder _____

The Albemarle Room set for a formal dinner

4 Language study   Describing use

Look at this example:

▶ *A video recorder **is used for recording** programmes from the television. It can also **be used for playing** back programmes.*

Write down five items of equipment found in a hotel room or in a conference room. As quickly as you can, get your partner to guess these items by making sentences like:

It is used for . . .
It can be used for . . .

Talking about contents

Look at these ways of talking about the contents of a room:

a *It's got*   *a flip-chart and a video.*
b *It contains*
c *It's equipped with*
d *It's set out*   *in boardroom-style/for a cocktail party.*
e *It's arranged*

1   Make questions that can be answered by the sentences above.
    Example:
    a *What has the room got?*

2   In pairs, look at the room you are in. Make sentences about the contents using the language above. When you have finished, ask your partner about the contents of their room at home.

Describing size and dimension

Look at these ways of talking about size and dimension:

a *It's 6 metres **wide** and 12 metres **long**.*
   *It's 6 metres **by** 12 metres.*
b *It's square/rectangular/round.*
   It's L-shaped.
   It's shaped like an H.
c *It **has a seating capacity of** sixty.*
d *It **can take up to** sixty people.*

1   Make questions that can be answered by the sentences above.
    Example:
    a *How big is it?*

2 Divide into pairs, **A** and **B**. Look at the following room plans.

A
Choose one of the rooms, but don't tell **B** which.

B
Ask the questions in **1** to find out which room **A** is thinking of.
Now swap roles.

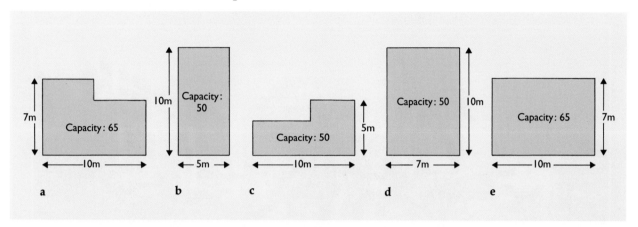

5 Speaking   Divide into pairs, **A** and **B**. **A**, your instructions are on page 146. **B**, your instructions are on page 150.

6 Reading   1 Divide into groups, **A** and **B**. You are each going to read a different section of a leaflet about the Abela Hotel, a conference hotel in Monaco.

A
Read your section about the general facilities of the Abela Hotel and the 'Conference Package'.

Make notes about:

a location and design of the hotel
b staff and service
c facilities in the hotel
d facilities in the rooms
e special features of the 'Conference Package'

B
Read your section about the social events which can be provided after conference sessions.

Make notes about:

a special welcome offers
b sporting activities available
c excursions and sightseeing trips
d evening entertainment

Abela Hotel
——— Monaco ———

Today's technology, traditional standards, and hospitality at its best.

The Abela Hotel, its architectural lines as agreeable as the view overlooking the Princess Grace rose garden, lies right on the sea front. To enter the lobby with its marble, pastel shades, and discreet lighting, is to appreciate modern luxury and traditional splendour. A warm welcome is the order of the day. The cheerful and efficient staff anticipate your every need, and the service is second to none. Being the perfect hosts, we have reserved one floor exclusively for non-smokers. There is an elegant Brasserie, evening music in the lobby-bar, a gift and newspaper shop, a shuttle bus service, and a multitude of other services at your disposal. True Monaco-style luxury at three-star prices! Your room will delight you with its cool, fresh décor, cable television, electronic mini-bar, and individual air-conditioning. To us, traditional hospitality is achieved through discreet efficiency and comfort. What could be better after an afternoon shopping or long hours in the conference room?

THE CONFERENCE PACKAGE

Includes

* ★ Air-conditioned conference room with natural light.
* ★ Baize table coverings; flip-chart.
* ★ Mineral water on the table during work sessions.
* ★ Note pads and pens.
* ★ Hospitality desk with direct-dial telephone on request.
* ★ Two coffee breaks: coffee, tea, and orange juice served.
* ★ 3-Course Lunch: entrée, main course, dessert. Wine, mineral water, and coffee included.

The Abela Extras

A Co-ordinator will be on hand at all times to ensure the success of your conference. We will take care of all your transfers, and make any arrangements you like for excursions, leisure activities, and evening events.

B

The most successful conferences happen at the Abela Hotel Monaco

The Abela Hotel Monaco invites you to try a fresh approach to business: work hard in the morning, unwind in the afternoon. We will lay on all the facilities and technical assistance you may need for your conference sessions. Then let us put together some special afternoon events – using our extensive knowledge and experience of what this exciting region has to offer ... and ensuring you enjoy it to the full!

A Smile of Welcome

* Helicopter transfer from Nice Airport.
* A 'welcome' cocktail – 'Le Bienvenue'.
* Room gifts for guests:
    - a bottle of fine wine
    - a half-bottle of champagne
    - a basket of fruit
    - local souvenirs: list on request.

Target: Sport

* A 4 x 4 off-road safari.

   Leave Monaco and head up into the Italian villages just over the border before tackling some rough forestry tracks. Return through the spectacular gorges of the Roya Valley.

   Picnic supplied by the Abela Hotel. Expert supervision guaranteed.

* Sport for all.

   A 45-minute coach ride takes you to a major sports centre where guests can participate in any (or all) of the following: tennis tournaments (or coaching), table tennis, volleyball, petanque, mountain biking, 4 x 4 off-road driving, triathlon events (cycling, swimming, and running). Experienced coaching staff are on hand. Lunch is available at the centre.

* Climbing (an introduction).
* Mountain biking.
* Water sports: sailing, windsurfing, parascending.

Target: Sightseeing

* Helicopter flights along the coast.
* Excursions aboard luxury, air-conditioned coaches to take in the local sights: the old village of Eze, the port of Villefranche, Saint Jean Cap Ferrat and the Rothschild Foundation, Beaulieu and the Villa Kerylos ... inland or by the coast ... there's plenty to catch the eye.

Target: Entertainment

* A wine and cheese party.
* Musical dinner parties with menus, table decorations, and music themed together: Classical, Provençal, Italian, Gypsy, New Orleans, Lebanese, Caribbean ...
* Floor shows: Lookalikes, Robotics, Illusionist, Dancers ...
* A Monaco 'Treasure Hunt' with questions supplied and prize presentation at dinner.

2   In pairs, one person from group **A** and one person from group **B**, look at these three groups who are thinking of holding their conference at the Abela Hotel. Use the notes you have made to discuss in what ways the Abela is suitable or unsuitable for them.

> **a**   Conference of UK Hoteliers and Caterers
>
> They want:
>
> luxury rooms and facilities with as many little extras as possible (they are used to very high standards).
>
> organizational arrangements to be made by the hotel as they do not have their own full-time conference organizer.
>
> some social events, but nothing too energetic. Simple sightseeing tours would be enough.

> **b**   Conference of Sales Managers of a manufacturing company (with partners)
>
> They want:
>
> a comfortable conference room, suitable for presentations and discussions.
>
> an active social programme of events during the day for non-participants. Note: the average age of delegates and partners is thirty-two.
>
> exciting evening events (with dancing, etc.). Food should be good, but is not a priority.

> **c**   Conference of French Wine Appreciation Society
>
> They want:
>
> an excellent restaurant with high-class French cuisine. The wine-list must be excellent (although they may possibly be able to provide their own).
>
> local tours which explore the history and geography of the local area.
>
> pleasant surroundings (for example, views, decor). The rooms themselves can be simple, but must be comfortable with good facilities. Note: the average age of the participants is fifty-five.

Compare your opinions with other pairs.

3 Look back at your texts on pages 114 and 115 and find a word or phrase which means each of the following:

A

a carefully designed to have an effect without being noticed
b the best
c to be used only by
d available and ready for you to use
e if you ask for it
f available

B

a provide
b if you ask for it
c very impressive
d to include the nearby attractions
e a lot of things to see

7 Listening

Look at this programme for the Hoteliers' Annual Conference to be held at a hotel in Edinburgh.

Hoteliers' Annual Conference, Edinburgh
Provisional Programme

Friday	16.00	Registration and check-in
	16.30	Introduction in main auditorium
	16.45-17.15	Opening address: Marjorie Willis, Chairperson of the British Tourist Association – 'The Tourist Industry in the 21st Century'
	18.30	Cocktail reception
	19.30	Dinner
Saturday	8.30	Breakfast
	9.30	Workshops (x3)
	11.00	Coffee
	11.30	Workshops (x3)
	13.00	Buffet lunch
	14.30	Optional excursion: Guided tour of the city and surrounding countryside (by coach)
		or Delegates may make use of the hotel swimming-pool and leisure centre and other hotel facilities
	19.30	Grand Conference Dinner
		Speech by Sir Norman Weston MP
Sunday	8.30	Breakfast
	9.30	Workshops (x3)
	11.00	Coffee
	11.30	Closing session: Basil Carter – 'Marketing Strategies to Promote Your Hotel'
	12.45	Summing up and closing remarks
	13.00	Buffet lunch and departure

---

1 Listen to a conference co-ordinator discussing the programme with her assistant. Make a note of the things which have been changed from the original programme.

2   Listen again and make a list of all the things which still have to be checked and arranged.

8 Activity

Imagine you are planning the details of the Hoteliers' Annual Conference looked at in *7 Listening* of this unit.

In groups, decide on subjects for the three sets of workshops. There should be three workshops at each time (in other words, nine workshops in all). Also decide what seating arrangements you want, and what equipment you need.

Complete this chart:

Workshop time	Title	Seating style	Equipment
Sat. 9.30–11.00			
1			
2			
3			
Sat. 11.30–13.00			
1			
2			
3			
Sun. 9.30–11.00			
1			
2			
3			

Are there any other changes you would make to the conference programme?

When you have finished, show your programme to another group.

9 Activity

It is the opening night of a new hotel and conference centre (the New Grand). A special reception party is being held. You are all characters at the reception.

Your teacher will tell you which of the characters you are.

Manager of the New Grand You are naturally very nervous and concerned that everyone is happy. Make sure that guests are not left on their own.

Assistant Manager of the New Grand You are proud of the new hotel and want to impress everyone, especially the Director.

Restaurant Manager of the New Grand You are worried that people haven't eaten all the food you have prepared.

Local tour guide You are desperate to make contacts because you are freelance and haven't had much work recently.

Manager of the Old Ship Hotel As the manager of a nearby hotel, you are worried about loss of business.

Catering goods supplier You are marketing a new range of quality hotel foods and want to attract this important new customer.

Conference and Banqueting Manager You are very proud of the hotel's conference facilities. Conference business is expected to account for the majority of the New Grand's trade.

Airline company executive You are interested in expanding your business into the hotel sector and you are looking for a deal with the new hotel.

Tour operator You are responsible for sending tourists to this area every summer. You are not happy with the other hotels and want to find a better one which will also give you a better deal.

Director of Grand Hotels You are one of the directors of the hotel chain, but you were not happy with the plan to build the New Grand. You are not sure it's going to be profitable. You have some doubts about the Manager, too.

Manager of the local Tourist Board You want to improve the image of the town and develop new services and attractions for tourists.

Local business person You are interested in the hotel as a possible venue for conferences for your company. You want to know exactly what the hotel can offer.

1 When you are given your role, write your name and job title on a badge. Then prepare your role by thinking about these questions:

   a Why am I here at the party?
   b What do I want to get?
   c Who could I talk to in order to get it?
   d Is there anyone I want to avoid?

2 Now act out the role play.

10 Writing

You are going to write a leaflet describing and promoting a conference hotel.

Choose one of the conference groups from *6 Reading*, **2**. Decide what they need and are looking for. Then decide where your hotel is located, how large it is, what it can offer, and any other information you consider important.

Write a leaflet designed to attract your conference group. Follow the structure of the Abela Hotel leaflet if you want.

a   general description of the hotel:
its location
its design and décor
hotel facilities
room facilities

b   details of a 'Conference Package' of special deals and facilities

c   explanation of local attractions and activities for delegates

You can also use some of the key expressions used in the Abela Hotel leaflet.

Examples:
traditional hospitality
a warm welcome
We will take care of . . .

11 Vocabulary

at your disposal p. 114, available and ready for you to use
Autocue p. 110, machine that allows a speaker to read words while looking at his/her audience
baize p. 114, thick (usually green) woollen cloth used for covering billiard tables, card-tables, doors, etc.
capacity p. 112, the greatest amount that a space can hold
discreet p. 114, carefully designed to have an effect without being noticed
exclusively for p. 114, only to be used by
goods p. 119, things for sale
lay on p. 115, provide or supply a service
lectern p. 110, sloping surface for holding a book or papers when reading in public
lecture p. 110, talk or speech to a group of people on a particular subject
on hand p. 114, available
on request p. 114, if you ask for it
press conference p. 110, interview given to journalists in order to announce a decision, an achievement, etc.

product launch p. 110, formal introduction of a new product
public address (PA) system p. 110, electrically-controlled apparatus for making a speaker clearly heard by large groups of people
second to none p. 114, the best
seminar p. 110, short business meeting at which working methods are taught or discussed
sessions p. 109, meetings
slide projector p. 111, apparatus which shows pictures on a screen
spectacular p. 115, very grand and attractive
speech p. 110, formal talk given to a group of people
video recorder p. 110, machine which is connected to a television, on which you can record or play back a film or programme
workshop p. 110, small meeting to discuss and learn about a particular subject

Anglo-Global Holidays plc

Specialists in holidays for young people (teenagers and students), primarily from the US, Canada, Israel, and Europe. Incoming groups and individuals are offered a full package of sightseeing activities, social events, and contacts with local youngsters, under the guidance of experienced youth workers. (Established 1957)

Brit-Tours Ltd

Deals in large volumes of group traffic from North America, specializing in complete incentive programmes plus special-interest groups and business conferences. Creativity and quality assured. US office in Dallas, Texas.

Hollywood Travel Services Ltd

Catering for both groups and individuals from all over the world, Hollywood Travel offers special interest tours in over eight different categories. Private entertaining in rural hotels and private houses of historic and architectural importance. Private shooting and fishing packages. The personal touch for an exclusive clientele.

Blue Skies Travel Ltd

An organization which sends over 80,000 people a year on short-stay packages, mainly to London. Specialists in concerts with coach travel, accommodation, and guided tours included. Contact through newspaper advertising throughout the UK. Also markets theatre programmes for schools.

Customtours Ltd

Custom-made itineraries, designed to meet the needs of both groups and individuals. Specializing in special-interest tours, performing groups, and youth groups from overseas and within the UK.

1 Reading

Tour operators are an important part of the tourism industry and, for many hotels, are a vital source of business, as they bring large groups.

Look at the pictures and read the profiles of the tour operators. Decide which picture goes with which tour operator.

2 Listening

You are going to listen to George Webber, who works for a large tour operator, talking about 'familiarization trips'.

1 Read through the questions below, then listen and make notes.

   a What is a familiarization trip?
   b How is it different today from the past?
   c Which travel agencies get invited on most of George's fam trips?
   d Which other agencies might get invited on 'new-product' trips?
   e Who pays for fam trips?
   f When will George be sending people on them?

2 After listening, discuss what questions you would put on a fam trip questionnnaire to make sure that travel agency employees used their time well. Make a list.

3 Language study   Future Continuous

We use the Future Continuous:

as a polite way of asking about somebody's plans.

   ▶ ***Will you be sending** people out soon?*

to talk about what we expect to happen.

   ▶ *We'll **be sending** people out in early May.*

1 Make questions using the following prompts.

Example:
You want your friend to give Jim a message. (you/see/Jim/tonight?)
Will you be seeing Jim tonight?

   a You want to lock up the office, but one of your colleagues is still working in there. (you/finish/soon?)
   b You are booking a guest into your hotel. (How long/you/stay?)
   c You want your friend to buy you some stamps. (you/go/post office/on your way home?)
   d You want to borrow your friend's typewriter. (you/use/your typewriter/this evening?)

2 Complete these sentences about plans using **will + -ing**.

Example:
I (work) all day tomorrow, so I won't have time to meet you.
I'll be working all day tomorrow, so I won't have time to meet you.

   a They (repeat) the performance on Thursday night, if you missed it this time.
   b He (come) back for a visit next month.
   c Jo (move house) on Sunday, so she can't come to the party.
   d We (travel) through London on Saturday, so we could meet you there.

Future Perfect

We use the Future Perfect to talk about an action that will already be completed by a time in the future:

▶ *By June, we'll have arranged some trips for the end of the summer.*
▶ *When will you have finished your work by?*

Combine the following sentences using the Future Perfect.

Example:
We are redecorating this wing. It will be ready by the middle of next year.
We'll have redecorated this wing by the middle of next year.

a The Dutch guests are leaving today. They will leave by twelve noon.
b The chambermaid is cleaning the room. It will be done by the time they arrive.
c The hotel hopes to double its business. It should manage to do so by the year 2000.
d The delegates have received the information. I am sure they will all read it before the start of the conference.
e The painters are doing the downstairs rooms now. They say they will finish by Friday.
f I have five letters to write. I plan to write them all before I go home.

Reported speech

Notice how we report statements:

'Fam trips **are** an opportunity for people to get to know **our** hotels,' said George.
▶ *You said earlier that fam trips **were** an opportunity for people to get to know **your** hotels.*
'**We've asked** everyone to fill in a questionnaire,' George told us.
▶ *George told us **they had asked** everyone to fill in a questionnaire.*

Now report the following statements in a similar way:

a 'We enjoy staying here,' said Thomas.
b 'We didn't have much time to relax,' Peter told us.
c 'The Browns are leaving at eight o'clock,' said Beatrice.
d 'We've lost your address,' Debby told us.
e 'It's been raining for hours,' said Frank.
f 'I don't remember where I left my keys,' Ronny told his wife.
g 'They will be here at any minute,' said Mary.
h 'I'll help you when I've finished,' Tony told them.
i 'I can't understand your handwriting,' Ian told me.
j 'You should apply for this job,' David told Catherine.

4 Reading

The Yorkshire and Humberside Tourist Board (YHTB), in conjunction with local Yorkshire hotels, Shearings (a major UK coach tour operator), and North Sea Ferries, has put together a familiarization trip for employees of NSF and OLAU, a Dutch tour operator.

1 Look at the map and itinerary and trace the route they will be taking.

Shearings Fam Trip Proposed Itinerary

Friday 23 October	TIME	
Arr. Harrogate	17.00	By this time at Cairn Hotel, Ripon Rd, HG1 2JD
	19.00	Assemble for YHTB presentation & to meet local tourism interests inc. other Shearings hoteliers
	20.00	Pre-dinner drinks
	20.30	Dinner and overnight at Cairn Hotel
Saturday 24 October		
Dep. Harrogate	08.30	Via A59 Knaresborough, Green Hammerton, York, A1036 to A64 Malton, Staxton to Scarborough
Arr. Scarborough	10.15	Coffee at Norbreck Hotel, Castle Rd, YO11 1HY
Dep.	11.00	Via A165 Burniston, Cloughton, A171 to High Hawsker, Whitby Abbey
Arr. Whitby Abbey	11.40	Visit Abbey & Parish Church, walk down 199 steps into Old Town
	12.55	Rejoin coach at New Quay Road by Tourist Information Centre
	13.00	Lunch at Royal Hotel, West Cliff, YO21 3HR
Dep. Whitby	14.00	Via B1410 Esk Valley to A169 and minor road to Goathland
Arr. Goathland	14.20	Brief stop at this 'heartbeat' village
Dep.	14.50	Via minor road to A169 Pickering, Malton and A64 to minor road to Castle Howard
Arr. Castle Howard	15.45	Castle Howard. View house & gardens
Dep.	16.45	Via minor road to A64, A1036 into York, A59 Green Hammerton, Knaresborough to Harrogate

Arr. Harrogate	18.00	Cairn Hotel
Dep.	19.15	Via A59
Arr. Knaresborough	19.30	Yorkshire Lass, Harrogate Road – pub for 'Yorkshire Neet'
	20.00	Dinner
Dep.	23.00	A59 to Harrogate
Arr. Harrogate	23.15	For overnight at the Cairn Hotel

Sunday 25 October

Dep. Harrogate	09.00	A61 to Ripley
Arr. Ripley	09.45	Ripley Castle, HG3 3AY. View Castle
Dep.	10.45	Via A61 and minor road to Fountains Abbey
Arr. Fount. Abbey (West Car Park)	11.05	View Abbey, Studley Royal Park and coffee, Fountains Hall
Dep.	12.15	Via minor road to B6265, Ripon, Bridge Hewick, Boroughbridge, Green Hammerton, A59 via Knaresborough back to Harrogate
Arr. Harrogate	13.15	Cairn Hotel for farewell lunch
	14.30	ENDS

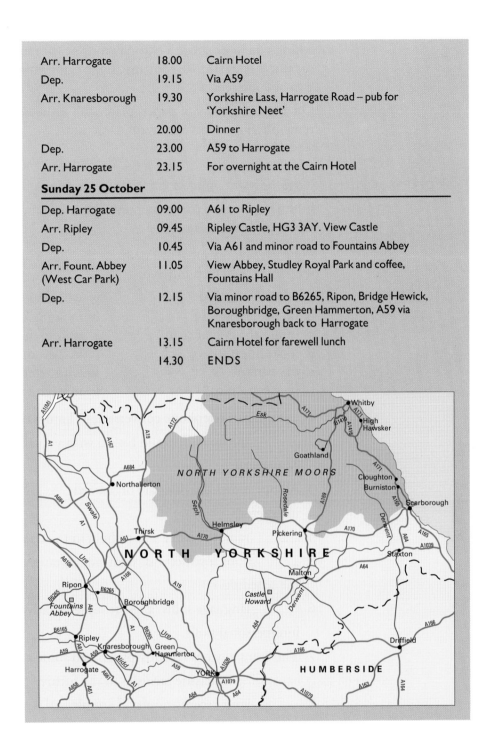

2 **a** Which hotels will the group be visiting?

   b What other places of interest will the group be going to?

   c What do the abbreviations *Arr.*, *inc.*, and *Dep.* mean?

   d In what ways will the various organizations which are involved benefit from this particular familiarization trip?

5 Speaking

You and your partner work for the local tourist board. Mr Edward Legrand, the Director of a tour operations company, has written to you asking you to organize a two-day tour of your area for him. His company organizes educational, sporting, sightseeing, and special-interest tours as well as conferences.

On a separate sheet of paper, plan a full itinerary for Mr Legrand, remembering to leave him some free time.

6 Word study

'*Organizations invest in fam trips **in the hope of** securing extra business.*'

in the hope of is a common prepositional phrase (preposition **in** + noun **the hope** + preposition **of**).

Put each prepositional phrase from the following list in its correct space in the sentences which follow.

a in the process of	g with a view to
b on behalf of	h in accordance with
c under the guidance of	i in response to
d in addition to	j in view of
e in terms of	k with reference to
f in the event of	l in payment for

1 ＿＿＿＿ our telephone conversation, I am writing to confirm our order.

2 ＿＿＿＿ the hotel, I would like to wish you a Happy New Year. (The Manager.)

3 All our sports activities are organized ＿＿＿＿ a fully qualified instructor.

4 ＿＿＿＿ rain, the party will be held in the conservatory.

5 ＿＿＿＿ your instructions, we have rearranged the meeting for later in the schedule.

6 ＿＿＿＿ language skills, a resort representative must have good interpersonal skills.

7 The company has recently purchased some adjoining land ＿＿＿＿ expanding its leisure facilities in the future.

8 ＿＿＿＿ your recent enquiry, I am pleased to inform you . . .

9 ＿＿＿＿ the current economic situation, we can expect fewer visitors this year.

10 The hotel has had some bad reviews but ＿＿＿＿ sales, it has been very popular.

11 We are ＿＿＿＿ negotiating a new contract with our tour operator.

12 I enclose a cheque ＿＿＿＿ our accommodation.

7 Listening

Diane MacLennan runs UK Hosts, a company which specializes in selecting hotels in London for incentive tours from the USA. An incentive tour is a reward or an encouragement for people who have done good work for their company. The companies she deals with are usually very rich. On the tape you will hear her being interviewed about her work.

1   Before you listen to Diane talking, try to guess what kind of hotel her groups look for.

2   Listen and check.

3   Read through the statements below, listen again, and complete the sentences using the information on the tape:

   a Diane depends upon her _____ to help her recommend appropriate hotels for her clients.

   b Diane's clients usually make an _____ of the hotels she has recommended.

   c It is _____ for her to visit fourteen hotels in one day.

   d For her groups, the three most important areas in a hotel are the _____, the _____, and the _____ .

   e Hotels keep Diane up-to-date by _____ and by _____ .

   f Trade magazines are useful for information about _____ .

   g To meet people in the industry she goes to _____ .

   h Diane _____ inspects the hotels she recommends.

8 Activity

Divide into pairs, **A** and **B**.

A

You are a tour operator. You are going to interview a hotel manager to see if the hotel meets your company's requirements. Read the extract below, then decide exactly what requirements your company has before you start the interview.

B

You are a hotel manager. Read the extract below and decide exactly what facilities you have to offer in your hotel. See if they meet the tour operator's requirements.

THE BUSINESS OF TOURISM

The hotels

In addition to operators spelling out their exact requirements in terms of rooms – required numbers of singles, doubles, twins; with or without private facilities; whether with balconies or seaview; and with what catering provision, e.g. rooms only with breakfast, half board or full board – they must also clarify a number of other issues. These include:

- reservations and registration procedures (including issue of any vouchers);
- accommodation requirements for any representatives or couriers (usually provided free);
- handling procedures and fees charged for porterage;
- special facilities available or needed, such as catering for handicapped customers, or special catering requirements (kosher, vegetarian, etc.);
- languages spoken by hotel staff;
- systems of payment by guests for drinks or other extras;
- reassurance on suitable fire and safety precautions;
- if appropriate, suitable space for a representative's desk and noticeboard.

It is also as well to check the availability of alternative hotel accommodation of a comparable standard in the event of over-booking.

Ancillary services

Similar negotiations will take place with locally-based incoming operators and coach companies to provide the coach transfers between airport and hotels and any optional excursions. Car hire companies may also be approached to negotiate commission rates on sales to the

Source: J. Christopher Holloway: The Business of Tourism

9 Activity

It takes a lot of careful planning, negotiating, administration, and marketing to put together a new tour programme. You are going to put together a summer holidays brochure featuring twenty to thirty hotels in different Mediterranean countries.

Using the tour-planning diary below, decide:

in what order it will be best to do each stage listed below.
what exactly will be involved in each stage.
why it will make sense to do them in that order.

a   estimate the exact selling prices based on exchange rates
b   negotiate with airlines and hotels
c   decide on destinations, hotels and capacity, duration of tours, and departure dates
d   finalize the reservations system
e   sign contracts with hotels and airlines
f   send first tours to resorts
g   distribute promotional material to agencies including brochures
h   start production of brochure
i   make an in-depth comparison of potential destinations
j   send final tour prices to printer
k   identify a likely selection of countries, resorts, and hotels
l   start advertising

TOUR-PLANNING DIARY

	J	F	M	A	M	J	J	A	S	O	N	D
YEAR 1							1			2		
YEAR 2	3	4		5		6	7	8	9		10	
YEAR 3	11			12								

10 Reading   Read the letter below from the Managing Director of the Hotel Sebastopol. Fill in the gaps with the correct word from the list:

attract, addition, inform, leaflet, facilities, popular, sending, offer, attracting, unknown, appearance, located

---

HOTEL SEBASTOPOL

Bedhilon
48600 Grandrieu
Lozère, FRANCE

Tél: (33) 230016
Télécopie: (33) 231889

23 March 199__

Underhill Holidays
Broadview Apartments
1800 30th Street
Boulder
Colorado 80391
USA

Dear Sir

Having seen your new 'Eurobreaks' brochure, we are writing to
1_____ you that we would be very interested in 2_____ your
company to this area of France and to our hotel, in particular.

We are 3_____ in an area which we believe would be very
4_____ with American tourists, but which is relatively 5_____.
We manage to 6_____ visitors from Canada and Australia but so far
there are no American operators 7_____ people to the area.

In 8_____ to the beautiful countryside, we have fishing, hiking, and
plenty of outdoor sports activities on 9_____. We find that our
Australian and Canadian guests really appreciate the French
countryside, particularly in summer. Our hotel is one of the largest in
the region and boasts 130 rooms, all with en suite 10_____. To give
you a clearer idea of the hotel's 11_____, I enclose an up-to-date
12_____ with full colour illustrations.

We look forward to hearing from you.

Yours faithfully

Christian Dessenon

Managing Director
HOTEL SEBASTOPOL

11 Writing

Your seaside hotel has decided it would like to attract more Austrian tourists. You have seen the brochure of an Austrian company and feel your hotel would be ideal for inclusion.

Write a letter to the tour operator explaining in detail the attractions of your area, saying what your hotel has to offer, and suggesting a time of the year when tourists might like to visit your hotel.

12 Vocabulary

alternative p. 128, different

assemble p. 125, meet

boasts p. 130, is proud to say it has

catering (for) p. 128, providing food and drink (for)

catering for p. 128, providing what is needed by

conservatory p. 126, room with a glass roof and walls

custom-made p. 121, specially made for the customer

evolve p. 168 (tapescript), develop

fam(iliarization) trip p. 122, trip which informs people about resorts

freebie p. 167 (tapescript), thing given away free

group traffic p. 121, groups travelling

guidance p. 121, control and supervision

in the event of sth p. 128, if sth happens

in-depth p. 129, detailed

incentive tours p. 168 (tapescript), tours organized by a company for its staff

incoming p. 121, arriving

inspects p. 127, looks at carefully

itinerary p. 125, plan of a journey

kept updated p. 169 (tapescript), always given the latest information

know intimately p. 168 (tapescript), know extremely well

leaflet p. 130, printed, usually folded piece of paper that gives information

mailing list p. 169 (tapescript), list of names and addresses of people to whom advertising material, etc. is to be sent regularly ▶

◀ **mailshot** p. 169 (tapescript), piece of advertising material sent to potential customers by post

National Trust p. 125, organization in the UK that takes care of beautiful places and historical buildings

on the line p. 169 (tapescript), at risk

outdoor p. 130, outside

overbooking p. 128, reservations for too many guests

performing groups p. 121, groups of entertainers

precautions p. 128, things that you do in advance to avoid possible danger or problems

preliminary p. 168 (tapescript), coming before something else which is more important

promote p. 168 (tapescript), publicize to encourage the success of

promotional p. 129, which promotes

questionnaire p. 123, list of questions answered by many people, used to collect information

socializing p. 169 (tapescript), mixing socially with other people

spelling out p. 128, explaining clearly and simply

tour operators p. 167 (tapescript), companies which produce package tours

tourist board p. 124, office that promotes an area or a country

up-to-date p. 127, most recent, current

vital p. 169 (tapescript), essential

Tour operation – execution

1 Listening

Donald Carter, the Front Office Manager of the Fir Tree Hotel, and a new trainee Assistant Manager, Peter Makeland, are waiting in the Group Check-in Lounge for a group to arrive.

Listen to the tape and, playing the role of Peter, complete the group check-in list below:

The Fir Tree Hotel

GROUP CHECK-IN LIST

Group name __Endo Group__

Passport list collected _____
Yes/No _____

Tour leader's name and room no.

_____

Voucher collected _____
Yes/No _____

Checked in by

_____

Food & Beverage bleep answered by

_____

Group rooms allocated by
__Reception Manager__

Additional remarks

_____
_____
_____

Rooms:

Single __27__

Twin __10__

Triples __2__

Suites __—__

Total __39__

_____
_____
_____
_____

Rooming list to

_____

Supervisor's signature

_____

2 Language study   Second Conditional

Look at what the tour guide says:

▶ *Three of our group are friends, and **they'd be** happier **if they shared** a room.*

Notice how the Second Conditional is formed:

If + Simple Past, would + Infinitive.

Put the verb into the correct form.

Example:
If you worked harder, you *would pass* your exams.

a If we had more money, we _____ (spend) our winters abroad.

b If he _____ (read) the newspaper every day, he'd know what was going on in the world.

c I suppose you think that if you were rich you _____ (be) happy.

d How much would you get if you _____ (sell) your car?

e If it _____ (not/rain) so much, I'd ride my bike to work.

f If they _____ (provide) a better service, they'd get more customers.

g They _____ (save) money in the long run if they employed their own maintenance people.

h I'd sack him if I _____ (not/think) he was doing the job well.

Reported questions

Notice how we report questions:

'Does Mrs Endo smoke?' asked Peter Makeland.
▶ *Peter Makeland **asked whether** Mrs Endo **smoked.***

'Can we share a room?' the three girls wanted to know.
▶ *The three girls **wanted to know if** they **could** share a room.*

'What time will breakfast be?' Megumi asked.
▶ *Megumi **asked what time** breakfast **would be.***

Now report the following questions in a similar way:

a 'Which room is the meeting in?' enquired the group leader.
b 'Where does this bus go?' Kevin wanted to know.
c 'Why aren't the rooms ready?' she asked me.
d 'When did the group arrive?' asked the manager.
e 'What time will the meeting finish?' asked Peter.
f 'Will the Japanese group be staying for dinner?' asked Helen.
g 'Shall I call back later?' Ian wanted to know.
h 'Have you written everything down?' asked Donald.

3 Speaking

You are a tour operator with a very varied clientele. Read the information below about three different groups and decide what possible/probable preferences they will have.

Consider:
type of hotel: de luxe, conference, etc.
board: bed and breakfast, half-board, etc.
room: type, location, facilities, services, extras.
use of facilities: conference rooms, function rooms, restaurants, etc.
optional tours: theatre, sightseeing, museums, shopping, etc.

Group 1
A group of students on an educational and cultural tour (mainly staying with families, but including some nights in a hotel).

Group 2
A group of elderly people visiting your capital city on a weekend package, including a visit to a variety show and a night in a hotel.

Group 3
A group of people of various ages on a cycling holiday.

4 Reading

Read this Welcome Letter and itinerary for a special group staying at the Copthorne Tara Hotel in London and answer the questions which follow.

UNIVERSITY OF SOUTH CAROLINA

WELCOME TO LONDON!

Enclosed with this letter you will find a map of London and general information which I hope will be of use during your stay.

Today you will be taken direct to your hotel where assistance will be given with check-in. The remainder of the day will be free for you to relax after your flight, for shopping or independent sightseeing. The programme during your visit will be as shown below. Departure of all tours and transfers will be from the Groups Lounge on the ground floor of the hotel.

The University of South Carolina Hospitality Desk, situated in the Groups Lounge, will be staffed for four hours from arrival for any assistance or information you may require or if you wish to book the optional tours. There will be someone to assist at the following times during your stay:

Thursday   5 March - Four hours from arrival
Friday   6 March - 1.00 p.m. - 5.00 p.m.
Saturday   7 March - 12.30 p.m. - 4.30 p.m.
Sunday   8 March - 8.00 a.m. - 12.00 p.m.
Monday   9 March - 8.00 a.m. - 12.00 p.m.
Tuesday   10 March - 8.00 a.m. - 12.00 p.m.

Breakfast is included daily and will be served in the Brasserie on the ground floor of the hotel between 7.00 a.m. and 10.30 a.m.

Friday, 6 March 199_
9.00 a.m. Depart for an optional meeting tour of the City of
           London. Afternoon at leisure.

Saturday, 7 March 199_
9.00 a.m. Depart for a morning tour of London's West End, included
           for everyone. Afternoon at leisure.

Sunday, 8 March 199_
8.30 a.m. Depart for an optional full-day Bath and Stonehenge tour.

Monday, 9 March 199_
9.00 a.m. Depart for an optional morning Windsor tour.
           Afternoon at leisure.

8.00 p.m. Evening at the theatre included for everyone. The
           performance of the musical '5 Guys Named Moe' commences at
           8.00 p.m. at the Lyric Theatre, Shaftesbury Avenue. Please
           make your own way to and from the theatre by taxi or tube
           (nearest station Piccadilly Circus). ▶

◄   Tuesday, 10 March 199_
       8.30 a.m.   Depart for an optional full-day Oxford and Stratford tour.

       Wednesday, 11 March 199_
       Departure details will be shown on the hospitality board at the
       University of South Carolina hospitality desk.

       10.15 a.m. Flight US 1161 departs for Charlotte.

       I hope you have a very enjoyable stay and look forward to welcoming
       you back to London in the not too distant future.

       Yours sincerely,

       Sue Hadow

       Sue Hadow
       Travel Co-ordinator

1 a What do guests receive on arrival?
b Where is the usual 'meeting point' for the group during their stay?
c Why is the hospitality desk not open on Saturday morning?
d Which meals are included in the cost?
e On which days are they completely free to do what they want?

2 Find formal words or expressions in the text which mean:

a help (verb)   **c** leave   **e** begins
b the rest   **d** free   **f** soon

3 If you were a student from the USC, which of these tours would you go on?

5 Word study

In the Welcome Letter in *4 Reading*, we read that 'the hospitality desk will be staffed for four hours from arrival'. This means that a member of staff will be there for four hours after the group arrives.

Below, there are some examples of formal written language which might be seen on the hospitality board of an inclusive tours group. Explain each sentence in a less formal way.

a Enquire at Reception for further details.
b Itinerary subject to alteration at short notice.
c Non-refundable deposit payable at time of reservation.
d All rates subject to VAT.
e Smokers are requested to refrain from smoking in communal areas.
f No gratuities to staff.
g Optional tours subject to adequate demand.
h Special rates available for OAPs.
i Lunch voucher valid on stated days only.
j The management reserves the right to refuse admission (notice outside hotel disco).

6 Listening

We asked Richard Tobias of the British Incoming Tour Operators Association (BITOA) to tell us about recent changes in incoming tour operations (tours of foreign visitors to the country, in this case, the UK).

1 Before you listen, look at the sentences below. Tell your partner whether the things mentioned have or have not happened in your country recently.

If you do not know, guess or try to find out!

a ☐ There has been a trading-up of accommodation from three-star hotels to four-star (tourists are staying in a higher standard of hotel).

b ☐ There are more five-star hotels.

c ☐ Hotels will negotiate more on prices.

d ☐ Standards of service are lower.

e ☐ There are more complaints about accommodation.

f ☐ There are more second-time visitors (people who have been to the country before).

g ☐ Heritage tours (tours which look at the traditions and cultural achievements of a country) are becoming more popular.

2 Now listen to Richard Tobias and tick (✓) the sentences if these changes have happened in the UK, and put a cross (✗) if they have not.

7 Reading

Look at the rooming list sent to the guide escorting the Koala Tours 'Sydney Opera' group and answer the following questions.

a Where is the group staying?

b How many rooms are required altogether?

c How many groups of three or more are there? What size are they?

d Who has the concert tickets?

e Who probably has difficulty with stairs?

KOALA TOURS

15 Cook Road, Sydney
Tel. No. Reservations 2-226-3150
OPERATIONS 2-226-6079
ACCOUNTS 2-226-9596

```
RX/SOP1/14119-/01
LEADER DRABBLE
HYLODGE HOTEL, SYDNEY
SYDNEY OPERA
14 NOV. 199__ 1 Night.
```

```
                              ROOMING LIST
    DOUBLE WITH FACILITIES
      CC MR/MRS B DOLAMORE
      CC MR/MRS A WILLIAMS
                        2 DOUBLE WITH FACILITIES  -  4 PAX


    TRIPLE WITH FACILITIES
      LF MISS J TATTUM/ MRS F TATTUM
         MRS D HUGHES
                        1 TRIPLE WITH FACILITIES  -  3 PAX


    SINGLE WITH FACILITIES
         DRIVER HAS TIX
                        1 SINGLE WITH FACILITIES - 1 PAX


    TWIN WITH FACILITIES                SPECIAL REQUESTS
      AA MR/MRS ROBERTS                 FS    FRONT SEAT REQUESTED
      AA MR/MRS BAKER                   LF    LOW FLOOR REQUESTED
         MRS N BANKS/MRS S JONES        AA    TRAVELLING TOGETHER (AA)
         MR/MRS L DUNBAR                BB    TRAVELLING TOGETHER (BB)
         MRS DYMENT/MRS W NOYES         CC    TRAVELLING TOGETHER (CC)
      DD MRS M ELSON/MRS T MULLEN       DD    TRAVELLING TOGETHER (DD)
         MRS FLETCHER/MRS K COUSINEAU
         MRS J M GRANT/MISS J GRANT     TOTAL - 50 PAX
         MRS J GRIFFITHS/MRS V MULLEN
         MRS J HILL/MISS R HILL         KOALA TOURS GUIDE (COACH ONLY)
         MRS W HUGHES/MISS S HUGHES
         MRS M MORRIS/MISS S MORRIS     TOTAL ON COACH - 51
         MRS J MACDOUGALL/MRS N JONES
         MR/MRS M ROBERTS
      FS   MISS M ROBERTS/MISS E WILLIAMS
      DD MRS B SCOTT/MRS K WILLCOCK
         MRS S TAYLOR/MRS J RAVENSCROFT
      BB T EVANS/G DAVIS
      BB MRS J THOMAS/J BURKE
      BB M PUMFORD/K WILLIAMS
      BB A NEEDHAM/J NEEDHAM

                21 TWIN WITH FACILITIES - 42 PAX
```

8 Activity

Read the job advertisement and decide which activities a resort representative would spend *a lot of* time doing and which activities he/she would spend *not much* time doing.

Booking Tours has a vacancy for a
RESORT REPRESENTATIVE
at El Sol, Cliff Top, & Esplendida Hotels, Majorca

THE WORK INVOLVES:
greeting incoming guests — hosting welcome parties — handling general enquiries — organizing and supervising social activities at the hotel — acting as a mediator with hotel staff, police, or other local authorities — advising guests on shopping — organizing optional excursions — ensuring all bills and taxes are paid — accompanying returning guests to airport for return flight to UK.

Experience preferred, but training given
For further information contact: **Susan MacDougal, Booking Tours, 132 Knapp St, Basingstoke, Hants, RG21 3PW**.

Working in groups, copy and complete the table below for three very different candidates for the Resort Representative job. They should be of equal ability to do the job (quite good), but they must be completely different from each other.

No candidate should be better than the other two candidates at more than *four* factors.

	Michael Rogers	Silvia Gonzalez	Jorge Diaz
age			
nationality			
languages			
education			
work experience			
present job			
hobbies/skills			
sports/fitness			
personality			
appearance			

Now pass the completed table to another group of students. Look at another group's table and discuss who should be given the job.

9 Activity

Tour operators often canvass holiday-makers for their opinions on their holidays. The results of the holiday surveys are shared with the providers of the relevant services.

Although your hotel has been operating successfully for twenty years, this is your first season using a mass-market tour operator. As far as you are concerned, it has been a great success.

At the end of the high season, you have received the preliminary results of their holiday surveys for your hotel.

Discuss the following in groups:

a your overall reaction to the results,
b the aspects of your hotel which *meet* the requirements of this kind of operation and those which *do not*,
c the possible reasons for your problems and the steps you can take to rectify them.

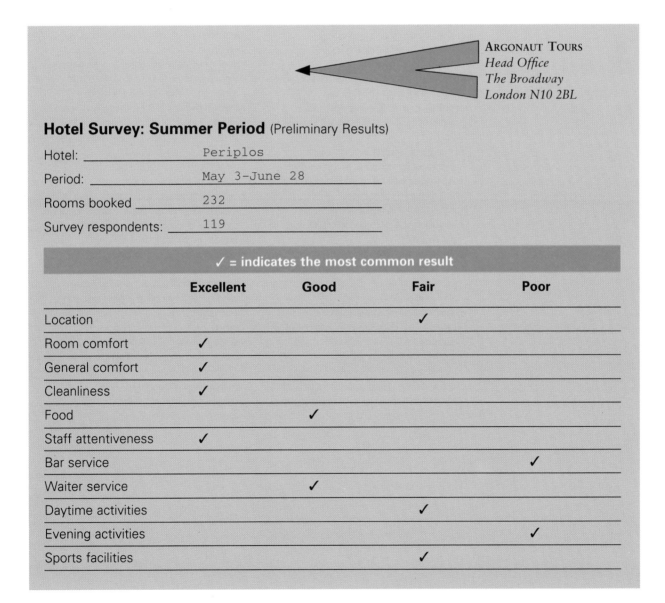

ARGONAUT TOURS
Head Office
The Broadway
London N10 2BL

Hotel Survey: Summer Period (Preliminary Results)

Hotel: _____ Periplos _____

Period: _____ May 3–June 28 _____

Rooms booked _____ 232 _____

Survey respondents: _____ 119 _____

✓ = indicates the most common result			
Excellent	**Good**	**Fair**	**Poor**
Location		✓	
Room comfort ✓			
General comfort ✓			
Cleanliness ✓			
Food	✓		
Staff attentiveness ✓			
Bar service			✓
Waiter service	✓		
Daytime activities		✓	
Evening activities			✓
Sports facilities		✓	

10 Writing

Write a letter to your British tour operator thanking them for the holiday survey preliminary results. Point out why you feel the tours have been a great success and why next year will be even better. Also, suggest reasons why some results were a little disappointing and explain what steps you will take to remedy any problems.

11 Vocabulary

accompanying p. 140, travelling with

assist p. 135, help

attentiveness p. 141, helpfulness and politeness

bleep p. 133, short, high-pitched sound made by an electronic device to call sb

canvass p. 141, find out the opinions of

cost effectiveness p. 171 (tapescript), giving enough profit compared to money spent

discernible p. 170 (tapescript), noticeable

driving a hard bargain p. 171 (tapescript), insisting on the best possible price, arrangements, etc. when negotiating with sb

escorting p. 138, going with

gourmet p. 171 (tapescript), serving fine food

heritage p. 138, the traditions and cultural achievements of a country

hospitality board p. 135, notice board which gives information

hosting p. 140, being in charge of

in-bound p. 170 (tapescript), coming to this country

leisure p. 135, free time

local authorities p. 140, people who are responsible for the local government of an area

major items of expenditure p. 170 (tapescript), things that most money is spent on

mass-market tour operator p. 141, one who sells very popular holidays

mediator p. 140, person who acts as a go-between for two people or groups who cannot or do not want to communicate directly

package p. 136, inclusive tour

private function rooms p. 136, rooms for private meetings, parties, etc.

profit margins p. 171 (tapescript), difference between the price at which you sell something and its cost

recession p. 170 (tapescript), period when the economy is not very successful

rectify p. 141, put right sth that is wrong

remedy p. 142, put right sth that is wrong

resort representative p. 140, person who works for a tour operator and looks after its guests in a hotel

rooming list p. 139 (tapescript), list of guests' names and their rooms

savour p. 171 (tapescript), eat slowly and enjoy

survey p. 141, study of people's opinions, behaviour, etc.

trading-down p. 170 (tapescript), exchanging something for something else of a lower standard; opposite **trading-up** p. 138

transfers p. 135, transport to the airport

travel co-ordinator p. 135, person who organizes travel arrangements

vacancy p. 140, job which has not been taken

variety show p. 136, light entertainment consisting of a series of acts, e.g. singing, dancing, comedy

are willing to do sth p. 171 (tapescript), do not mind doing sth

Pair/Group A
Instructions

Waiter role-card

Congratulations! You have just got your first job as a waiter at a high-class restaurant.

In the role play you will be able to show how good you are at the job. Make notes in the table below before you start.

Stage 1	What to say and do
1 greet the customers 2 take customers' coats 3 seat customers at a table 4 offer a drink 5 bring menu and wine list 6 take orders	
Stage 2	What to say and do
1 bring first course 2 collect empty plates 3 bring main course and serve vegetables 4 ask if everything is OK and pour more wine 5 collect plates and bring sweet trolley (and serve) 6 offer coffee and anything else 7 bring bill (when asked) 8 give customers their coats and say goodbye	

Unit 8   4 Speaking   [p. 92]

You are a representative of the Charleston Tourist Information Office. The passage that follows contains information about attractions and tours in Charleston. Answer the visitor's questions and give advice on what to do. If the passage does not contain some of the information that the visitor requests, be prepared to invent it.

HISTORIC HOUSES AND MUSEUMS

Calhoun Mansion * – beautiful example of a typical Victorian Charleston house; wonderful interior and fittings (especially ballroom). $10 admission.

Heyward-Washington House – lovely old house built in 1772; pretty garden and kitchen area. $4 admission.

Gibbes Museum of Art – American art from the 18th century to the present. $2 admission.

The Old Exchange and Provost Dungeon – Built in 1771, this contains the original trading floor of the Exchange, and the dungeon where British officers imprisoned American patriots. One of Charleston's most historic places. Open 9–5 daily.

TOURS

Charleston Carriage Tour – horse-drawn tour round the historic area (with guide).

Gray Line Bus Tour * – luxury coach tour of old town and surrounding areas (with guide).

Tea Party Walking Tour – guided tour on foot, including tea in a private garden.

Talk of the Towne – comprehensive sightseeing coach tours, including the only tour that visits the famous Nathaniel Russell House.

LOCAL AREA

Magnolia Plantation – old slave plantation, beautiful house with lovely garden and small farm/zoo. $12 admission.

Fort Sumter – old fort; site where the American Civil War began; boat trip and guided tour included. $9 admission.

USS Yorktown * – aircraft carrier and other warships; ideal for kids. $8 admission.

* highly recommended

Unit 8   9   Activity   [p. 97]

LEEDS CASTLE, CANTERBURY, AND DOVER

We begin at Leeds Castle, set on an island in the middle of a lake and surrounded by ª_____ _____. It became known as Lady's Castle, because of the number of Queens of England who lived there. Today, many people say it is the loveliest castle in the world and it is used for ᵇ_____

_____ between heads of state. Leeds Castle is also renowned for its unique museum of dog collars.

Canterbury and its Cathedral

Canterbury is England's ecclesiastical capital, where St Thomas Beckett, then Archbishop of Canterbury, was murdered in ᶜ____ by the knights of ᵈ_____. Beckett's shrine in the Cathedral became the goal of the 'Canterbury Pilgrims' and the town prospered on this early form of tourism. Bypassing the queue, we enter the Cathedral, which was founded as a monastery by St Augustine in 597 and was enlarged in both the 11th and the 14th centuries.

The White Cliffs of Dover

Our final port of call is the port of Dover, renowned for its great stretch of white chalk cliffs. We visit 12th century Dover Castle – designed by Henry II but incorporating much Norman architecture – and from the ramparts we may see the coast of France. Leaving Dover, we return to London, travelling past the Channel Tunnel entrance and workings, making our first drop-off at around ᵉ_____.

Highlights

- Visit Leeds Castle
- Visit Canterbury Cathedral
- Visit Dover Castle
- View Tunnel entrance
- All entrance fees paid

Departures		Days	Price
Blakemore Hotel:	8.05 am	Tuesdays	Adults
136 Wigmore Street:	8.10 am	Thursdays	£ ᶠ____
Victoria LTB:	8.10 am	Saturdays	
Trafalgar Square:	8.15 am		Children
Park International:	8.20 am		£ 34.50
Royal Albert Hall:	8.45 am		(3 - 17 yrs)

Plus direct pick-ups from over 35 hotels. Ask your concierge for details.

Unit 10   5 Speaking [p. 113]

1 You have a plan of the Chesterfield Suite where you and your partner are holding a conference. You have the dimensions, the seating style, and the equipment available in each room. Your partner has an outline plan with none of this information and will ask you questions to obtain it.

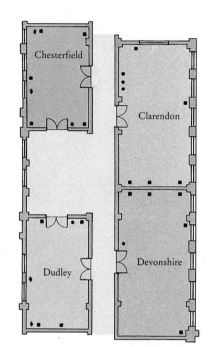

C h e s t e r f i e l d · C l a r e n d o n · D e v o n s h i r e · D u d l e y

	Chesterfield	Clarendon	Devonshire	Dudley
Size	5.3 m x 7.6 m	5.5 m x 10.5 m	5.5 m x 10.5 m	5.3 m x 8.4 m
Style	Boardroom	Theatre	Schoolroom	Boardroom
Capacity	14	40	24	14
Equipment	video	OHP + screen	flip-chart	slide projector

2 You have an outline plan of the Spencer Suite. You need the dimensions, the seating style, and the equipment available in each room. Your partner has this information. Ask him/her questions and complete the grid below.

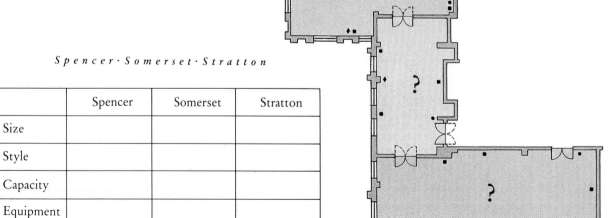

S p e n c e r · S o m e r s e t · S t r a t t o n

	Spencer	Somerset	Stratton
Size			
Style			
Capacity			
Equipment			

Pair/Group B
Instructions

Unit 1

10   Activity   [p. 18]

You are the representative for a group of beach resort hotels. A tour operator has phoned you to check the names of a number of hotels that he/she wants to include in the summer brochure. Listen to your partner's descriptions and try to match them with the named hotels below. Ask questions to check, if necessary.

Question prompts:
Has it got . . .?
How many . . .?
Is there a . . .?/Are there any . . .?
What shape is . . .?

Lido

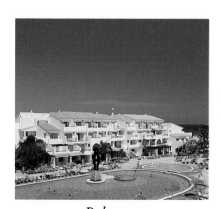

Bahamas

Grand

Anemi

Sol Milanos

Beverley

Dassia

Unit 7   10   Activity   [p. 86]

Customer role-card

You and the other customers are really restaurant inspectors dining incognito. It is your job to see how waiters can cope with the pressures of the job. As a team you have to work out the best way of testing each waiter. There are various ways in which this can be done. You can be angry, rude, drunk, talkative, difficult to please, loud, etc.

It is very important that the waiters do not realize who you are. Be like a normal customer at first.

It is best if you save most of your good ideas for Stage 2 of the role play. Make notes in the table below before you start.

Stage 1	What to say and do
1 arriving and being seated 2 pre-dinner drink 3 menu and ordering	
Stage 2	What to say and do
1 first course and wine 2 main course 3 dessert trolley 4 coffee 5 the bill 6 leaving	

Unit 8   4   Speaking   [p. 92]

You are a visitor to Charleston. You need as much information as possible from the Tourist Information Office. Ask for advice on:

the historical houses and museums – the cheapest/best value, but also the most typical
the best way to tour the city
attractions in the surrounding area
shops
restaurants and nightlife

9 Activity [p. 97]

LEEDS CASTLE, CANTERBURY, AND DOVER

We begin at Leeds Castle, set on an island in the middle of a lake and surrounded by beautifully landscaped gardens. It became known as Lady's Castle, because a_____ _____. Today, many people say it is the loveliest castle in the world and it is used for top-level conferences between heads of state. Leeds Castle is also renowned for its unique museum of b_____.

Canterbury and its Cathedral

Canterbury is England's ecclesiastical capital, where St Thomas Beckett, then Archbishop of Canterbury, was murdered in 1170 by the knights of Henry II. Beckett's shrine in the Cathedral became the goal of the 'Canterbury Pilgrims' and the town prospered on this early form of tourism. Bypassing the queue, we enter the Cathedral, which was founded as a monastery by St Augustine in c____ and was enlarged in both the 11th and the 14th centuries.

The White Cliffs of Dover

Our final port of call is the port of Dover, renowned for its great stretch of white chalk cliffs. We visit 12th century Dover Castle – designed by Henry II but incorporating much Norman architecture – and from the ramparts we may see d_____. Leaving Dover, we return to London, travelling past the Channel Tunnel entrance and workings, making our first drop-off at around 6.15 p.m.

Highlights

- Visit Leeds Castle
- Visit Canterbury Cathedral
- Visit Dover Castle
- View Tunnel entrance
- All entrance fees paid

Departures		Days	Price
Blakemore Hotel:	e_____	Tuesdays	Adults
136 Wigmore Street:	8.10 am	Thursdays	£ 38.50
Victoria LTB:	8.10 am	Saturdays	
Trafalgar Square:	8.15 am		Children
Park International:	8.20 am		£ f_____
Royal Albert Hall:	8.45 am		(3 - 17 yrs)

Plus direct pick-ups from over 35 hotels. Ask your concierge for details.

Unit 10   5   Speaking   [p. 113]

1   You have an outline plan of the Chesterfield Suite where you and your partner are holding a conference. You need to find out the dimensions, the seating style, and the equipment available in each room. Your partner has this information. Ask him/her questions and complete the grid below.

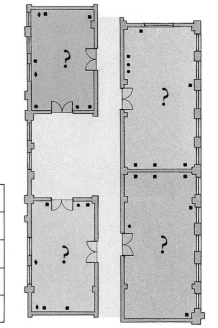

C h e s t e r f i e l d · C l a r e n d o n · D e v o n s h i r e · D u d l e y

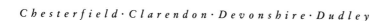

	Chesterfield	Clarendon	Devonshire	Dudley
Size				
Style				
Capacity				
Equipment				

2   You have a plan of the Spencer Suite. You have the dimensions, the seating style, and the equipment available in each room. Your partner has an outline plan with none of this information and will ask you questions to obtain it.

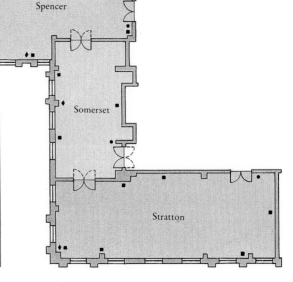

S p e n c e r · S o m e r s e t · S t r a t t o n

	Spencer	Somerset	Stratton
Size	5.6 m x 12.0 m	5.3 m x 11.0 m	6.0 m x 16.6 m
Style	Schoolroom	Boardroom	Theatre
Capacity	24	20	60
Equipment	flip-chart + whiteboard	TV + video	PA system OHP + screen

Tapescripts

Unit 1

1 Listening

1 I travel a lot – up to three months a year – so I guess you could say I spend a quarter of my life in hotels! For me, the ideal hotel has big rooms with comfortable beds and good facilities – including a business centre. It should also be as near the centre of town as possible, but within easy reach of the airport.

2 I love going on vacation, especially in Europe. I worked hard all my life, so I feel I deserve a little luxury now – and I don't mind paying for it. If you ask me, a hotel that doesn't make you feel really special isn't a hotel!

3 I like smaller hotels because you can learn more about the country, the people, and the culture. The staff have more time for you. I think most of the big hotels are so impersonal. They all look the same. When you are inside them, you can't tell which country you're in.

4 It's my job to visit hotels, not just the de luxe 5-star ones, but also the small family-run places with only a few rooms. But if you're asking me personally, the most important things are polite and friendly staff and efficient service. Anything else is really a bonus.

5 Listening

Dialogue 1

CTB: California Travel Bureau. Jenny speaking. How may I help you?

CALLER: Hello, yes, I'm going to California in the summer on a fly-drive holiday and hoping to spend some time in Yosemite National Park. Could you give me some information about accommodation?

CTB: Certainly. The first thing to say is that if you want to stay in a hotel you'll need to make a reservation pretty soon. Have you any definite dates?

CALLER: Well, we're arriving in San Francisco on 13th July and we'll probably spend a week there and then get to Yosemite around the 20th – probably stay about two or three days.

CTB: I see. And do you want to stay in a hotel or camp?

CALLER: Hotel, definitely. We don't need anything too luxurious – just a private bathroom, if possible.

CTB: How many in the party?

CALLER: Just two.

CTB: Well, there are three hotels. The Ahwahnee is quite expensive – around $200 a night. The two others are about the same price – approximately $75 a night. The Yosemite Lodge is very popular, so you'll need to make a reservation very soon. Or there's the Wawona, which is very pretty.

CALLER: I see. Could you possibly send me details?

CTB: Certainly. Could you give me your name and address?

CALLER: Yes. It's Ms Wallace, 14 Station Road, London N6.

CTB: OK, Ms Wallace. Is there anything else?

CALLER: No, I think that's all – thanks for your help.

CTB: You're welcome.

Dialogue 2

CTB: California Travel Bureau. Jenny speaking. How may I help you?

CALLER: Oh, hello. My name's Curtis. I'd like some information, please.

CTB: Certainly. What would you like to know?

CALLER: Well, I'm thinking of going to California with three friends this summer, and I've heard it's possible to camp in Yosemite National Park, but someone told me you have to reserve?

CTB: No, you don't have to reserve, but you have to get a permit. When exactly are you coming?

CALLER: Probably late July, early August.

CTB: In that case, you can get a permit for seven days in the valley and fourteen days out of the valley.

CALLER: Right. We're planning to do a lot of walking, so we'll probably go up into the mountains. Can we just camp where we want?

CTB: No, you have to camp in the designated areas, but if you go for the Type B sites, you'll find they're not too crowded. The facilities are pretty basic, but they only cost $4.

CALLER: Sounds good.

CTB: Would you like me to send you some information?

CALLER: Yes, that would be great.

CTB: OK, can I just have your name and address?

CALLER: Yes, it's Mr J. Curtis, Flat 2, 36 Wood Lane, Bristol.

CTB: OK, Mr Curtis, I'll put that in the mail for you.

CALLER: Thanks.

CTB: You're welcome. Bye.

Unit 2

2 Listening

JOHN: Hello, Peter!

PETER: John! How nice to see you! I haven't seen you for ages!

JOHN: No, not since I left the Palace. It must be four years. You're not still there, are you?

PETER: I'm the General Manager, actually.

JOHN: Well, well! Congratulations!

PETER: Thank you. What are you doing here?

JOHN: Oh, I'm still involved with hotels, sort of. I'm a partner in a company that builds leisure facilities – swimming-pools, saunas, tennis courts, that sort of thing. I can't interest you in a pool, can I?

PETER: I'm afraid you're too late. We've already got one. Yes, we've made quite a few changes since you were there. We built a large extension a couple of years ago with a pool, fitness centre, solarium, and sauna. We've even opened a couple of tennis courts. It's a pity we didn't know about you. We might have been able to give you some business.

JOHN: Well, I've only been there for a little over a year. But tell me, you must be doing pretty well, then?

PETER: Yes, things are a lot better than they were four years ago, that's for sure. You know there was a take-over about a year after you left?

JOHN: Yes, I heard.

PETER: Well, they've put a lot of money into the hotel, and it really looks great now. Our rooms are far more comfortable and we offer the best facilities in the area. So of course we can charge higher prices. It's certainly paying off – occupancy rates are right up!

JOHN: Well, it was about time. What about those old family rooms in the annexe?

PETER: Last year, we converted them into business apartments and a business centre.

JOHN: Really? Good idea. A lot of hotels are going that way.

PETER: We're hoping to open a suite of conference rooms in the next year or two.

JOHN: Well, the old Palace certainly sounds a different place!

PETER: Yes. We've expanded the restaurant, too.

JOHN: Who's the chef? It's not still Carlos, surely?

PETER: Heavens, no! He's gone back to Spain. No, in the end we hired a top French chef, Marcel Fauzet. Have you heard of him? He's been with us for more than three years now, and he's certainly made a difference. You must come and have a meal with us some time.

JOHN: Yes, I must. It's just a pity I can't sell you a swimming-pool!

5 Listening

Dialogue 1

CALLER: And what about the facilities within the rooms?

RECEPTIONIST: OK. The rooms are on the third floor overlooking the park. They are en suite with bath and shower in each. All our rooms have a colour television and telephone in them. There are coffee- and tea-making facilities. There's a mini-bar and trouser-press, too.

Dialogue 2

CALLER: What facilities do your rooms offer?

RECEPTIONIST: Well, the rooms you're interested in are quite unusual. First of all, let me say, they're on a split level. This means you go up to the sleeping area and then down again to the bathroom. They have beautiful crystal chandeliers and still have the original high ceilings from the time it was a country home. And, of course, they're fitted with all the necessary features of a modern luxury hotel.

Dialogue 3

CALLER: And what are the rooms like?

RECEPTIONIST: What are the rooms like . . . um, they're medium-sized to small, I suppose. They're traditional, . . . homely. There's plenty of wardrobe space and the ladies like them because they've got large full-length mirrors in each. What else can I say? Oh, well, the rooms facing south have a view of the bay. That's about it, I think.

Unit 3

1 Listening

1 Let me start by saying I'm the General Manager. That is to say, I have control over the whole of the operation. As the General Manager, I must make sure that all our hotels and business outlets are fulfilling the overall vision of the company as a whole, and making money, too. We mustn't forget that our aim is to make money.

The company structure works like this. The House Manager is directly answerable to me. He or she is responsible for all six in-house departments, and their job is to keep good information flows between the various departments. We cannot allow departments to be run in isolation of each other. They must also make sure that the hotel stays profitable. They have a great deal of freedom to make decisions and don't have to check with me about day-to-day issues, although we are in regular contact by fax. Of course, the House Manager should use his discretion about when to contact me.

In our organization, the Resident Manager has control over the customer-contact side of the business. It is the Resident Manager's job to ensure close, efficient liaison between the two sectors under his control, that is to say Front-of-House Operations and Housekeeping.

2 I'm the Front Office Manager. I report to the Resident Manager on a regular basis but I can make a lot of daily operational decisions myself. I like the responsibility the hotel allows me to have. I have to supervise Front-of-House Operations and to do that efficiently, I need to have the assistance of the Head Receptionist, who looks after the reception area in general and has a good deal of contact with both staff and guests. We're concerned with day-to-day issues such as guests' comfort and security, but we also get involved in training and staff development, so there's plenty to do on that side, too.

3 I'm hoping to become Head Housekeeper in the near future. I've been Housekeeper for the Executive suites for a year now and there's a good chance I'll take over when Mrs Jones leaves at the end of the year. At the moment, I give orders to the chambermaids and cleaners personally, but I'm looking forward to getting more involved in planning and training. I know I shouldn't say this, but I think I'll be pretty good at it.

6 Listening

In this organization, the Concierge's primary function is to provide for guests' needs and special requests. This often involves contacting companies for information or services which are external to the hotel. Typical requests are for him or her to make bookings for tours, theatres, and special attractions. The Concierge will also help guests to organize and book their onward travel arrangements, including dispatch of luggage. Consequently, there is a need to know what services local businesses have to offer. That means businesses such as restaurants, travel agencies, and car-hire agencies.

To do the job effectively, the Concierge must be particularly aware of the arrival and departure of groups and any special events taking place within the hotel. Internally, the Concierge Department is responsible for the safe delivery of mail and packages and they will maintain a supply of stamps for domestic and foreign postage. In some hotels, it is still a Concierge's duty to fulfil requests for secretarial work but here that comes under the remit of the business centre.

A log-book is kept in which all guests' queries and requests are recorded. This is another of a Concierge's many duties. A basic requirement that we have of our concierge staff is that they display a courteous and professional manner in all their dealings with guests and fellow employees. Above all, he or she must have a friendly personality. We lay particular emphasis on maximizing guest satisfaction. Therefore, a Concierge will endeavour to fulfil a guest's requests, if at all possible, and hopefully do it with a smile.

Unit 4

2 Listening

Dialogue 1

HOTEL: Hotel Melissa. Can I help you?

CALLER: Yes, I'd like to make a reservation, please.

HOTEL: I'll put you through to Reservations. Hold the line, please.

RESERVATIONS: Reservations, Peter speaking. Can I help you?

CALLER: Yes, I'd like to make a reservation.

RESERVATIONS: Certainly. What name, please?

CALLER: Lewis, David Lewis.

RESERVATIONS: Right, Mr Lewis, when would you like to stay?

CALLER: I'd like to reserve a double room for three nights from the 21st April.

RESERVATIONS: OK. 21st April, three nights, double. I'll just check availability . . . Yes, we can do that for you. Is this a company booking or an individual?

CALLER: Oh, it's individual.

RESERVATIONS: Have you stayed with us before?

CALLER: No, I haven't.

RESERVATIONS: Would you like one of our Executive rooms, Mr Lewis, on the top floors with some wonderful views?

CALLER: Well, actually, no, I wouldn't. My wife doesn't really like using the lift and also she's got a bad leg, so I was hoping we could have a room near the ground floor.

RESERVATIONS: OK. I'll make a note of that and when you check in the receptionist will allocate a room on the first floor for you.

CALLER: Thank you.

RESERVATIONS: Will you be paying by credit card?

CALLER: Yes, I will. It's Visa.

RESERVATIONS: And what is the number?

CALLER: Hold on . . . It's 4335 171 36094.

RESERVATIONS: So that's 4335 171 36094. And your address?

CALLER: 14 St John's Road, London NW6.

RESERVATIONS: OK, Mr Lewis, that's reserved for you. Your reservation number is PS1462. We look forward to seeing you on the 21st.

CALLER: Thank you.

RESERVATIONS: You're welcome.

Dialogue 2

HOTEL: Hotel Melissa. Can I help you?

CALLER: Good morning. I'd like to reserve a couple of rooms.

HOTEL: Certainly. I'll put you through to Reservations. Hold the line, please.

RESERVATIONS: Reservations, this is Peter speaking. How can I help you?

CALLER: Good morning. This is Rita King from Imperial Plastics. I'd like to reserve a couple of doubles for April 13th.

RESERVATIONS: Two doubles for April 13th . . . Right. Availability is fine for that night. Is that a company booking?

CALLER: Yes, Imperial Plastics. The rooms are for a Mr Suarez, spelt S-U-A-R-E-Z, and Mr Johansson, spelt J-O-H-A-N-S-S-O-N. They'd like the Executive rooms.

RESERVATIONS: OK. You have an account with us, don't you?

CALLER: Yes, we do.

RESERVATIONS: But the guests haven't stayed with us before, have they?

CALLER: No, I don't think so.

RESERVATIONS: And how is the account to be settled?

CALLER: Full bill on the company account.

RESERVATIONS: Can I just check your contact details? It's Miss R. King, Imperial Plastics, Old Dock Road, London E5.

CALLER: That's correct.

RESERVATIONS: Right, Miss King, the reservation number is PS43307. I would be grateful if you could just confirm in writing, by fax if you like.

CALLER: Certainly. Thank you for your help.

RESERVATIONS: You're very welcome. Goodbye.

8 Listening

RECEPTIONIST: Can I help you, sir?

GUEST: Hello, I'd like a room for the night.

RECEPTIONIST: Do you have a reservation?

GUEST: No, I don't.

RECEPTIONIST: OK. Just the one night?

GUEST: Yes.

RECEPTIONIST: And one person?

GUEST: One person, yes.

RECEPTIONIST: Would you like an Executive at £125 or a Standard at £95?

GUEST: Just a Standard.

RECEPTIONIST: OK . . . Do you have a preference for a twin or a double-bedded room?

GUEST: Twin, please.

RECEPTIONIST: Do you have a preference for smoking or non-smoking?

GUEST: Non-smoking, please.

RECEPTIONIST: OK. You're in room 760.

GUEST: OK.

RECEPTIONIST: How will you be settling your account, sir?

GUEST: Visa.

RECEPTIONIST: By Visa card. May I take an imprint of your Visa card?

GUEST: Here you are.

RECEPTIONIST: Thank you. And the name, sir, is . . .?

GUEST: Paul Smith.

RECEPTIONIST: And may I take your home address, please?

GUEST: It's 5383 Collins Avenue, Miami.

RECEPTIONIST: And do you have a zip code?

GUEST: 23892.

RECEPTIONIST: OK, sir. Because you're not a British citizen, I'll require your passport in order to complete the registration.

GUEST: Here it is.

RECEPTIONIST: Thank you very much.

GUEST: Does the rate include breakfast?

RECEPTIONIST: No, it doesn't. Breakfast is £7.50 for continental and £9.95 for English and is served in the Brasserie Restaurant on this floor from 6.30 all morning, or you can order in your room through room service at no extra charge.

GUEST: OK.

RECEPTIONIST: This is your registration card. Can you just check through the details, please?

GUEST: Yes.

RECEPTIONIST: And sign here.

GUEST: OK.

RECEPTIONIST: Thank you. Here's your credit card, passport, and here's your key. It's room 760 on the seventh floor. The elevator is on the right. If you just tell a porter your room number, he'll follow you up with the luggage.

GUEST: Thank you very much.

RECEPTIONIST: Enjoy your stay.

Unit 5

3 Listening

Dialogue 1

MAN: I've already decided what I want.

WOMAN: What's that?

MAN: I'm going to have the fondue. It's delicious here.

WAITER: I'm sorry, sir, the fondue's off.

MAN: Really? In that case, let me think – I'll have the pork medallions.

WOMAN: I think I'll have the same.

MAN: And we'll have a bottle of Chablis.

WAITER: Very well, sir. Thank you very much.

. . .

WAITER: Would you like any desserts?

MAN: Yes, I'd like the gâteau, please.

WOMAN: Just a coffee for me, please.

MAN: Make that two coffees.

WAITER: Thank you.

Dialogue 2

WOMAN: Could we possibly order, please?

WAITER: Certainly.

WOMAN: I'd like the délices de Grison, please, and the mixed salad, followed by the fondue.

WAITER: Sorry, the fondue's off tonight.

WOMAN: Oh. What do you recommend, then?

WAITER: The veal is very good.

WOMAN: Well, I'll have that, then.

WAITER: Very well, madam. And for you, sir?

MAN: I'll have the salmon mousse, I think.

WAITER: And to start, sir?

MAN: Nothing, thanks. Do you think you could bring us the wine list, though?

WAITER: Yes, of course.

. . .

WAITER: Are you ready to order dessert?

WOMAN: Yes. Could I have the parfait, please?

MAN: And I'll have the soufflé glacé au Grand Marnier.

WAITER: Certainly.

Dialogue 3

WAITRESS: Are you ready to order?

MAN: Yes, I think so. I'd like the Beef Madras.

WOMAN: Yes. Could I have the fish, please?

WAITRESS: What vegetables would you like?

WOMAN: Sauté potatoes . . . and peas, please.

WAITRESS: And would you like a starter?

MAN: Yes, I'll have the crudités.

WOMAN: And chicken liver pâté for me.

MAN: No, sorry, could you change mine, please, to melon and prawn cocktail?

WAITRESS: So that's no crudités?

MAN: No.

WAITRESS: The melon and prawn cocktail instead.

MAN: Yes.

WAITRESS: Fine.

WOMAN: And can you bring us a bottle of water, please?

WAITRESS: Certainly.

7 Listening

Dialogue 1

RECEPTION: Reception. Can I help you?

GUEST: Oh hello, this is Mrs Rogers from room 718. I'm afraid I've lost my watch – it's a Rolex, and very expensive. I think I may have left it in the sauna changing room – or maybe in the pool area.

RECEPTION: I see. Have you been back to look, Mrs Rogers?

GUEST: No, I haven't. I thought I'd try phoning first, but I can't find the number. Oh dear, I'm so worried . . .

RECEPTION: Don't worry, Mrs Rogers, I'm sure we'll find it. I'll put a call through to the sauna and pool attendants' office straight away. I just need a few more details. What's your room number again?

GUEST: 718.

RECEPTION: And can you describe the . . .

Dialogue 2

RECEPTION: Reception. How may I help you?

GUEST: Good afternoon. Could you possibly book a table for two in the restaurant for me this evening?

RECEPTION: Certainly, sir. Can you tell me your name and room number?

GUEST: Yes, it's Mr Price and the room is 226.

RECEPTION: OK, Mr Price. What time would you like the table for?

GUEST: Now that's the problem. We're going to the theatre, and we'd like to eat when we return – say 10.30?

RECEPTION: I'm sorry, sir, the restaurant closes at 9.30.

GUEST: Oh dear.

RECEPTION: I could order a late supper for you – it would be brought to your room.

GUEST: Yes, that would be nice – we'll only want something light in any case, and perhaps a bottle of something.

RECEPTION: All right, Mr Price. I'll contact the restaurant and have them prepare a supper for you for 10.30. What would you like? There's a choice of . . .

Dialogue 3

RECEPTION: Reception. Can I help you?

GUEST: This is Mr Higgins in room 308. I'm afraid I'm not feeling very well. Would you mind asking someone to send up some aspirin – I haven't got anything with me.

RECEPTION: I'm sorry to hear that, Mr Higgins. I'll have room service send up some aspirin immediately. Would you like the nurse to visit you?

GUEST: No, I think I'll be OK, dear. Just the aspirin.

RECEPTION: OK. But phone us if you have any problems.

GUEST: I will.

RECEPTION: It was room 308, wasn't it?

GUEST: Yes, that's right.

Unit 6

2 Listening

Dialogue 1

RECEPTIONIST: That'll be £37.20, please, sir. How would you like to pay?

GUEST: Oh, I don't know. Do you accept credit cards . . . or a cheque?

RECEPTIONIST: Yes, or it can be added to your bill.

GUEST: Oh, yes. Can I charge it to my bill?

RECEPTIONIST: Certainly, sir. What room are you in?

GUEST: Room 408. Here . . . here's my key card.

RECEPTIONIST: Right, thank you. That's fine. Could you just sign here, please?

GUEST: OK . . . Could you wrap them for me?

RECEPTIONIST: Of course. I can arrange for them to be sent as well, if you like.

GUEST: That's an idea – it'll save carrying them. How much do you charge?

RECEPTIONIST: Well, it's . . .

Dialogue 2

RECEPTIONIST: Good morning, madam. How can I help you?

GUEST: I'd like to check out, please.

RECEPTIONIST: Certainly, madam. I'll get your bill. What room are you in?

GUEST: 702.

RECEPTIONIST: Here you are, madam. Would you just like to check it through?

GUEST: Yes . . . Can you tell me what this item is for?

RECEPTIONIST: That was the morning papers you had.

GUEST: But I don't think I ordered any papers.

RECEPTIONIST: Didn't you? I'd better check the voucher . . . You're quite right. Those papers were sent to 703. I'm very sorry about that, madam.

GUEST: That's quite all right. Actually there's another thing: I didn't order anything from room service either. Do you think there's some mistake? Oh, look! I've been given the wrong bill – this is 703 not 702!

RECEPTIONIST: I'm awfully sorry.

GUEST: That's all right. I thought it was a bit odd.

RECEPTIONIST: Here you are. Miss Smith, isn't it?

GUEST: Yes. Ah, that looks better. Everything seems to be fine. Oh, there's just one last thing. I wasn't sure about service charges in the restaurant. Are they included?

RECEPTIONIST: Yes, madam.

GUEST: Good. I thought so.

RECEPTIONIST: How would you like to pay?

GUEST: Do you accept Visa?

RECEPTIONIST: Of course. If I could just have your card.

GUEST: Here you are.

RECEPTIONIST: Thank you . . . That's fine. I hope you have a pleasant journey.

GUEST: Thank you. Goodbye.

Dialogue 3

RECEPTIONIST: Hello, can I help you?

GUEST: Yes, I'd like to change some dollars. Can you tell me what the exchange rate is?

RECEPTIONIST: Cash or traveller's cheques?

GUEST: Cash.

RECEPTIONIST: Right, the rate is one dollar forty to the pound.

GUEST: OK. Is commission charged on that?

RECEPTIONIST: Yes, we charge a flat rate of £2 per transaction.

GUEST: OK. I think I'll change two hundred dollars. How much will I get exactly?

RECEPTIONIST: Right, sir, let me just calculate it . . . 200 divided by one point four equals . . . 142 pounds eighty-six less two pounds commission . . . That comes to 140 pounds and eighty-six pence.

GUEST: Good. That should be enough. Here you are . . .

7 Listening

INTERVIEWER: Do you have a fixed room rate?

RESERVATIONS MANAGER: In common with most large hotels, our room rate policy is quite complicated. We have a basic room rate for all our room types, but the way that we sell our rooms means that we often charge a different rate from this. This is because our Sales and Marketing Department has negotiated different rates with different agents, corporate clients, and other clients.

INTERVIEWER: What are your basic room rates?

RESERVATIONS MANAGER: Well, we have a Standard room which contains all the basic facilities, such as private bath, TV, tea- and coffee-making facilities, and the basic rate for the double is £85 a night. Our Luxury rooms, or Executive Plus as some of them are called, contain a little bit extra: they're a bit more spacious, have better views and so on – they're £115 a night. Then we also have suites, which vary a lot in price.

INTERVIEWER: What discounts do you offer on these basic room rates?

RESERVATIONS MANAGER: You mean discounts for the individual non-corporate booking? [Yes] Well, we have special weekend rates: two nights, either Friday/ Saturday or Saturday/Sunday will get a 10% discount. That's to encourage a two-night booking even though weekends can be our busiest time. And our weekly rate is calculated on the basis of seven nights for the price of six. That's on all room types.

INTERVIEWER: Can you tell us how the specially-negotiated room rates work?

RESERVATIONS MANAGER: Like most hotels of our size, individual bookings paying the full room rate are a minority. Most of our guests come through some other source, either as part of a tour, through a tour operator, or a corporate guest. We get lots of repeat guests from particular companies and they obviously have a contract with us. There's a corporate rate, but there are also special rates negotiated and arranged with the Sales and Marketing Department, who enter them onto the computer for the Reservation and Front Office to access whenever an enquiry or reservation comes in. In addition, a lot of our rooms are sold through agents and representatives: these are either Free Sale Agents or Allocation Holders.

INTERVIEWER: What exactly are Free Sale Agents?

RESERVATIONS MANAGER: Well, every week, or even daily at busy periods, we send out availability charts to Free Sale Agents, who are usually in the States or Europe, and are usually either part of our own company or reputable agents. They sell rooms at an agreed rate – normally the corporate rate – which is arranged by the Sales and Marketing Department. They are told every week what rooms they can sell and if they can sell at a discounted rate or not. The Free Sale Agent doesn't need to check with us first, so it lowers administration costs; they just send in a confirmation sheet.

INTERVIEWER: What about Allocation Holders?

RESERVATIONS MANAGER: Allocation Holders are agents who have a certain number of rooms that they agree to sell in our hotel. They normally sell on FIT rates – Fully Inclusive Tariff rates – which are from the leisure side of the business and are cheaper than corporate rates. The customer pays them directly, they get commission and pass on what is left to the hotel. The rate is agreed with the Sales and Marketing Department. An Allocation Holder usually has up to twenty rooms over a weekend, on a seventy-two hour release – in other words, by Wednesday, the hotel can take the rooms back and re-sell them.

Unit 7

3 Listening

Dialogue 1

RECEPTIONIST: Good evening. Can I help you?

GUEST: Well, I hope you can. I'm in room 607 and frankly, it's disgusting. I'm extremely annoyed.

RECEPTIONIST: Oh, dear. What exactly is the problem?

GUEST: Everything. For a start, the room is ridiculously small. I specifically requested a large room.

RECEPTIONIST: I see. Is there anything else?

GUEST: Yes, there is! It's absolutely filthy. Yesterday, when I arrived, it was dirty, and it's quite obvious that it hasn't been cleaned for days – the bath's got dirty marks all over it and there's dust everywhere.

RECEPTIONIST: Well, that's strange: they should have cleaned it this morning and yesterday. Are you sure?

GUEST: Of course I'm sure! I know dirt when I see it! And another thing: the sheets haven't been changed.

RECEPTIONIST: Oh, dear. I'll send room service up with some clean sheets, and I'll make sure the room is cleaned first thing tomorrow morning.

GUEST: Tomorrow! I'm afraid that's not good enough. I want it cleaned now, immediately, do you hear?

RECEPTIONIST: Well, I'm terribly sorry, but that's not possible. The cleaning staff have all finished now. You should have complained earlier.

GUEST: What? This is totally unacceptable! If you can't clean my room then I want to move.

RECEPTIONIST: I'm awfully sorry, but we're fully booked.

GUEST: I don't believe this. I demand to see the manager.

Dialogue 2

RECEPTIONIST: Good evening. Can I help you?

GUEST: Well, I hope you can. I'm in room 607 and frankly, it's disgusting. I'm extremely annoyed.

RECEPTIONIST: OK. Mrs Jenkins, isn't it?

GUEST: Yes.

RECEPTIONIST: Now, what exactly is wrong?

GUEST: Well, for a start, the room is very small – I requested a large room.

RECEPTIONIST: Actually, room 607 is one of our larger rooms.

GUEST: Is it? Well, I'm bitterly disappointed, I'm afraid. Also, it's very dirty: the bath hasn't been cleaned and the sheets haven't been changed.

RECEPTIONIST: Oh, I'm terribly sorry, Mrs Jenkins. It must be most upsetting for you. I'm quite sure there's been some mistake. I'll send someone up immediately to look at it.

GUEST: Well, really I'd like to move room now.

RECEPTIONIST: I understand. We are very busy, but I'll see what I can do. Why don't you wait in the lounge bar while I sort this out. I'll arrange for a complimentary drink for you.

GUEST: Well, OK, then.

RECEPTIONIST: I really am most sorry, Mrs Jenkins, for the inconvenience you've suffered.

9 Listening

WOMAN: I must tell you about this one hotel we stayed in, about three years ago.

FRIEND: Where?

WOMAN: Well, it was just a little place in the country. We went for our anniversary – thought it would be relaxing and romantic. We'd seen it advertised in a magazine and it looked really quiet and peaceful.

FRIEND: And wasn't it?

WOMAN: Well, not exactly, no! For a start, when we arrived on the Friday evening, there was no one at the desk, so we rang the bell and waited, but nobody came. Then we heard voices in the back room, shouting and getting louder and louder, so we rang the bell again and eventually this little red-faced man popped out and shouted, 'Yes? What do you want?'

FRIEND: Ha ha.

WOMAN: Well, we were a bit taken aback, but we explained we had a reservation and he calmed down and we checked in. He told us the room number – 106 . . .

FRIEND: You've got a good memory!

WOMAN: Well, there's a reason.

FRIEND: Oh.

WOMAN: Anyway, he gave us the key and off we went, only to find that the key didn't fit the door. It turned out that he'd given us the right key but the wrong room – we should have been in room 107.

FRIEND: And was the room OK?

WOMAN: Yes, it was fine – the bathroom was a bit small, but OK. There were no towels, though. I went down to ask for some and he just said, 'You want towels? You didn't bring one?' I was furious! Anyway, he apologized and brought us some.

FRIEND: Ha ha ha. Sounds awful.

WOMAN: Well, it doesn't end there! It went from bad to worse. Dinner was a disaster. The service was appalling. The waiter was drunk and could barely stand upright, let alone carry the food. He dropped my soup all over the floor. And the food was vile – tasteless and overcooked.

FRIEND: Did you complain?

WOMAN: We were sick of complaining! It was more trouble than it was worth. We just left and walked along the river to the local pub, which was lovely. But then we went back to the hotel to spend the night.

FRIEND: Oh no! What happened then?

WOMAN: We got back and went to bed. So far so good. But then after about ten minutes a horrible screaming noise started. We didn't know what it was. It sounded like someone being murdered, but we came to the conclusion it must be to do with the water pipes. Well, whatever it was, it went on all night and we hardly slept at all. By the morning we'd had enough. There was no way we were going to spend another minute there. We got our things together, had breakfast, which was surprisingly good, and asked for the bill. He got all upset and asked why we were leaving, at which point we complained about everything. He got really annoyed and said we'd have to pay for the second night because we'd made a reservation. Well, he eventually backed down after we threatened to write to the local tourist board and the local newspapers, but he still tried to charge us for some newspapers we never had.

FRIEND: Did you go to another hotel?

WOMAN: Oh no, we just gave up and went home. Our weekend was already ruined. But anyway, the final chapter in the horrible saga happened about a month later. I was reading the paper and I came across a story about a murder in a country hotel. Guess which hotel?

FRIEND: No!

WOMAN: Yes! There were photos of it plastered all over the paper. The hotel owner had killed his wife after a blazing row and hidden the body in one of the bedrooms. But a guest was given the wrong key by mistake and found the body by chance.

FRIEND: Oh no, that's horrible!

WOMAN: And worst of all: guess which room the body was hidden in.

FRIEND: Oh, not yours. I don't believe it.

WOMAN: Yes, number 107!

Unit 8

2 Listening

REPRESENTATIVE: Right, everyone. Now I want to tell you about some of the excursions you can go on. You don't have to stay by the hotel pool all day every day, you know! There's a lot to see on the island of Crete and we've arranged some very special excursions for you. I'm just going to tell you about some of them. On Monday, we have a trip called 'Cultural Crete', where we visit many of the different cultural sights on the island. If you come on this tour, you'll see one of the earliest examples of Minoan civilization at Phaestos, and also the Roman ruins at Gortys. On Tuesday, we have a trip called 'The Best of the West'. This is a coach tour along the coast to the west of the island, driving through some spectacular mountain scenery and stopping at two lovely Cretan towns – Rethymnon and Chania . . . Yes, madam?

GUEST 1: How much do these excursions cost?

REPRESENTATIVE: Well, 'the Best of the West' tour is 6,400 drachmas for adults and half-price for children. Now, we also have a trip to the ancient Minoan city of Knossos on Wednesday and on Saturday. This is one of the most famous archaeological sights. You can see the remains of the old palace and city – it's over 3,000 years old.

GUEST 2: What day did you say it was?

REPRESENTATIVE: Wednesday and Saturday. So, as I was saying, if you come on this trip you can experience some of the finest examples of Minoan culture. Also on Wednesday, we have a very special evening of Cretan dancing and drinking. We drive out to a little mountain village where the locals entertain us in the open air with some beautiful dancing and a light meal accompanied by the local drink, raki – don't drink too much of it because it's very strong!

The price of 5,700 drachmas for adults includes the meal and the drink. The coach will leave at six p.m. and we'll return around midnight.

GUEST 1: You said it's in the open air. What'll we do if it rains?

REPRESENTATIVE: Well, I don't think it's very likely to rain at this time of the year. But if it does rain, we'll go inside and eat in the restaurant there. Now, there's just two more trips I want to tell you about. The first is on Sunday and it's for those of you who are very strong and fit! It's called the 'Samaria Adventure'. It involves leaving the hotel at six o'clock in the morning on Sunday, and driving to the top of Samaria Gorge. You then have to walk seventeen kilometres through one of the most beautiful natural sights in Europe. You finish up many hours later at the beach and harbour where a ferry takes you along the coast and back to your coach. If you're fit and love adventure, then you'll love this trip. If you come, bring plenty of water and wear good strong shoes. Finally, a much more leisurely trip is the Santorini cruise which runs on Monday, Wednesday, Thursday, and Friday. It's a delightful boat trip to the impressive volcanic island of Santorini. You can have a donkey ride up to the town, eat lunch, do some shopping, and then return to the cruise ship in the evening, when there'll also be dinner served and dancing.

GUEST 3: What time do we get back?

REPRESENTATIVE: Probably about midnight. Now, here are the booking forms. If you have any questions, or if you want any advice, please ask me.

GUEST 4: Yes, I'd like to see some of the Minoan ruins, but I've heard there's a lot of walking and steps at Knossos, and I'm not very good at walking.

REPRESENTATIVE: Mmm. Well, why don't you come on the Cultural Crete excursion – there's not so much walking there and you still see lots of beautiful sights.

GUEST 3: Does it matter which day we go on the Santorini cruise? Is there any difference?

REPRESENTATIVE: No, the tour's the same on each day, but if I were you I'd wait till the Thursday or Friday. By that time you'll be more used to the sun; you're out in the sun quite a lot on that trip. You could always spend a day or two exploring the town here . . .

8 Listening

Good afternoon, ladies and gentlemen. My name is Jenny and I welcome you on this tour of historic Charleston. I'd like to introduce you to our driver, Tom.

Our tour today will take about three hours but we'll be stopping to visit a few places and to take photographs. It's a very hot day out there so we'll take it easy. As you can see, the coach is air-conditioned, but we can adjust it if you want. Anyway, let's begin. As we leave the hotel, we're driving down Meeting Street towards the river front. On your left is the Old Market and just coming up on your right is the Gibbes Museum of Art, which contains one of the finest collections of American paintings, prints, drawings . . .

Now as we pass this fine church on your left – St Michael's, the oldest church in the city, built in 1761 – we are in the centre of the Historic District. As you can see, virtually every house here is a fine example of southern architecture. These houses were nearly all owned by rich planters who came to Charleston and the coast in the summer to escape the heat and the mosquitoes of the back-country. If you look down to your left, you'll see the Heyward-Washington House, built in 1772 by Thomas Heyward, one of the men who signed the American Declaration of Independence . . .

OK, ladies and gentlemen. The river is now in front of us on the other side of this rather delightful park. On the left you can see the Calhoun Mansion, perhaps the finest of the Charleston historic houses, although it was built a little later, in 1876, as a Victorian showpiece. I'll tell you a little more about that in a moment, as we'll be stopping there soon. The park is known as the Battery, or, officially, White Point Gardens, and you can see examples of cannons and other war relics. Charleston was a very important military centre, especially during the War of Independence when the Americans fought many battles with the British fleet. We'll be getting off the coach in a moment and walking along the harbour wall to Calhoun Mansion, and from the wall you'll see many examples of this military and naval history – forts from the era of the War of Independence, and from more recent times the aircraft carrier USS Yorktown. OK, we'll get off now. Please stay with me. If we do get separated for any reason, we'll be meeting at the coach again in one hour's time at four o'clock at the Calhoun Mansion . . .

Welcome back. I hope you enjoyed the Mansion. It certainly is something special, I think you'll agree. We're now going to drive a little way out of the historic town and visit the Charles Towne Landing, which will be our final stopping-point for today . . .

We're now crossing over the Ashley River Memorial Bridge, and the Charles Towne Landing is just over there on your right. Let me tell you a little about it. This is the place where the first settlement was made in 1670. It has now been made into a large park with exhibits showing the colony's history, a recreation of a small village, all in a delightful wooded atmosphere . . .

We're now back at the hotel. If you want to visit some shops then King Street, the main shopping area, is just one block ahead of you. Thank you for your attention. I hope you enjoyed the trip, and I hope you all enjoy the rest of your vacation here in Charleston.

Unit 9

1 Listening

INTERVIEWER: Donald, you said that it is important to treat all your guests well, but differently. Could you explain what you mean by that?

DONALD: Yes, of course. Like any other company, we, as a hotel, need to be able to identify those customers who are important to us. Just as an airline will try to offer a better-quality service to first-class passengers, we'll try to provide a higher standard for our important guests. Business travellers, for example, generally expect a higher class of service. Also, because they are frequent travellers, business people are potential *regular* customers and it is very, very important for the hotel to attract regular guests. Some of our business clients have been coming here for years because, we like to think, we look after them well.

INTERVIEWER: So, are all business people treated the same?

DONALD: No, using the same logic, we like to distinguish between different types of business guests, too. Some have Very Important Person status, or VIP for short. A typical VIP guest might be a customer, like a company salesperson, who makes *regular* visits. The VIP business guest soon becomes well-known by all the front-of-house staff – indeed we have one Italian salesman who we see on almost a weekly basis! Then there is the CIP, who is a Company Important Person, which means he is an important person in a company which the hotel does a lot of business with. That might be a company that makes regular use of our conference facilities or business apartments, for example. Finally, top of the range is the VVP, or very, very important person, such as the managing director of an important company. Of course, not all managing directors are VVPs, and businessmen are not the only important people.

INTERVIEWER: So, how are they treated differently?

DONALD: Well, unlike the normal business guest, the VIP has his or her room allocated in advance. We make sure we have all the necessary information about the guest and his company on the computer. We'll know what kind of room he likes, what side of the hotel, and so on. So there's just a simple check-in procedure. The duty manager is made aware of the VIP's presence in the hotel, but he doesn't usually come out to meet him. For the CIP, the room is also allocated in advance. However, all CIP rooms are double-checked, to make sure that everything is OK, and some additional extras are usually included. For example, if a CIP has asked for something in the past, we try to make sure it's there again on his or her return. Again, check-in is very simple and the duty manager does try to meet the CIPs if at all possible.

INTERVIEWER: OK, so there's extra attention to detail.

DONALD: Right. Then, there's the VVP. Whereas CIP rooms are double-checked, all VVPs have their rooms treble-checked, the last check by the senior housekeeper or duty manager. What's more, a full range of extras is provided, including flowers, wine, chocolates, etc. For a VVP, there's no need to check in at Reception. The duty manager always meets and accompanies the guest to his or her room, where check-in procedures can be completed. In other words: for us, all our guests are important, but some guests are definitely more important than others.

5 Listening

INTERVIEWER: Margaret, can you tell us a little bit about yourself? I know you travel quite a lot in your job. Can you tell us about some of the business trips you go on?

MARGARET: Certainly. As Marketing Director, most of my travel is abroad as I'm working with agents, mainly in Europe, but also in Japan and Brazil. Many of the trips are exhibitions and conferences, but also sometimes I'll go off my own bat to visit agents or contacts that we have already made or are hoping to establish.

INTERVIEWER: How do you usually arrange these trips?

MARGARET: If it's a trade fair or exhibition then it will often come as a package, so the hotel, the stand, and the flight will all come together, but if I'm going on my own, then I would usually get my secretary to organize the flight and a hotel in a good location.

INTERVIEWER: Interesting. What type of accommodation do you stay in normally and what special features do you look for in a hotel?

MARGARET: I tend to look for a hotel close to the trade fair or centrally located if I'm having several meetings in the centre or outside the city. Basically, when I'm abroad I still need access to a fax and my own phone, but other than that it would be the normal en suite room, sports centre if possible, depending on how long I'm going abroad for.

INTERVIEWER: Do you need special secretarial services while you're abroad?

MARGARET: Sometimes, but mainly I can get by with hand-written faxes. Occasionally, if several letters have to be sent, I'll obviously make use of the secretary in the hotel.

INTERVIEWER: Because a lot of hotels nowadays do have Business Centres. Have you found those useful?

MARGARET: Definitely. Especially if you're on a long-haul trip or travelling around for two or three weeks, and you've got to report back to the office.

INTERVIEWER: Are there any special facilities that you look for as a business*woman*?

MARGARET: Well, number one has got to be the location. You want to be in a good part of the town, preferably easy to get taxis, or near a metro station. For security reasons I would always ask for a room near the lift and on one of the lower floors. I don't like spending a lot of time in a lift on my own or walking along long corridors, even when I'm in a city that's safe.

INTERVIEWER: Do you find that hotels treat you differently because you're a woman?

MARGARET: Often they presume that you're just staying there while your husband is at meetings, which is very presumptuous of them to begin with. But sometimes I don't think you get such good rooms as the businessmen although you pay exactly the same rate.

INTERVIEWER: Really? Now, I know you've visited many different countries, not just in Europe but also in Japan and South America. Have you been aware of different business customs and practices?

MARGARET: Well, certainly before travelling to another country, I always try to read up a little bit about how business is conducted there. For example, in Japan the giving and receiving of business cards is much more elaborate than it is here in Europe. Similarly, when you go to visit a Japanese office, the first thing they often ask you to do – especially in the smaller offices – is to take your shoes off and put on some slippers, at which point you're usually given a glass of green tea. I found that Japanese businessmen and women do make you feel very welcome, much more so than in some of the busier European offices, where you can be left waiting for your business appointment to turn up.

INTERVIEWER: Right. That's all very interesting. Thank you very much indeed, Margaret.

Unit 10

3 Listening

MANAGER = Conference and Banqueting Manager (Grosvenor House Hotel)

CO-ORDINATOR = Conference Co-ordinator (ETOA)

MANAGER: OK, before we go and look at the rooms, I'll just tell you a little bit about them. If you'd just like to look at this plan.

CO-ORDINATOR: Thank you. I'll make some notes, if you don't mind.

MANAGER: Sure. Now, I think the Albemarle Suite is going to be the most suitable for your conference.

CO-ORDINATOR: Yes, I thought so when I saw your brochure.

MANAGER: It's a very attractive suite. It contains four rooms in all – the Albemarle, the Aldford, the Apsley, and the Waterloo.

CO-ORDINATOR: Right. Now, we need one room larger than the others for our opening and closing meeting with all the delegates. That's the Albemarle, isn't it?

MANAGER: Yes, the largest room is the Albemarle and we usually have that arranged in theatre-style. It can take up to sixty people.

CO-ORDINATOR: Good. How big is it exactly?

MANAGER: Let me see . . . It's ten and a half metres wide and fourteen point two metres long.

CO-ORDINATOR: I see. Ten point five by fourteen point two. Thank you. And what was the seating capacity again?

MANAGER: Sixty.

CO-ORDINATOR: And does it have a public address system?

MANAGER: Well, it does, actually, although usually it's not needed because it's not that big a room. It's also equipped with a video recorder and a slide projector with screen.

CO-ORDINATOR: Good. What about the other rooms? Can you give me some details?

MANAGER: Well, there's the one next to the Albemarle – it's connected, in fact – that's the Aldford. It's five point six metres by eleven point eight, and we usually have that set out in schoolroom-style.

CO-ORDINATOR: What were the measurements again? It's not written on this plan.

MANAGER: Five point six by eleven point eight. It's a rectangular shape.

CO-ORDINATOR: And what equipment does this one usually have?

MANAGER: Normally an OHP and a whiteboard – although we can vary it, of course.

CO-ORDINATOR: Good. What about these other two rooms?

MANAGER: Well, there's the Waterloo Room. That's quite long and thin, four metres by ten point eight five, often used for smaller receptions. It's got a TV and a video. Then there's the Apsley Room, which is square-shaped, more or less. It measures six point one by seven point seven metres, and is very richly decorated. It makes a very nice boardroom. It's equipped with a flip chart and a video.

CO-ORDINATOR: OK, I think I've got notes on all that now.

MANAGER: Right, shall we go and look at them then?

CO-ORDINATOR: Sure.

7 Listening

CO-ORDINATOR: OK, let's just run through the arrangements as they stand at the moment. I've got the original draft programme here. Now, I know there have been a few changes.

ASSISTANT: Yes, and I'd like to check some of the arrangements, in any case.

CO-ORDINATOR: Well, registration is still at four o'clock. Have we received the name badges yet?

ASSISTANT: No, I don't think so. I'll make a note to check.

CO-ORDINATOR: And after registration they want to have tea provided in the foyer lounge. That means the opening address will begin at five o'clock, not quarter to.

ASSISTANT: We've got to make sure that Marjorie Willis keeps her talk brief – she's only got half an hour and she tends to go on a bit, I've heard.

CO-ORDINATOR: Yes, the delegates will need time to freshen up and change before the reception and the dinner – and those times are fixed. Now, one thing – at dinner we've been asked to ensure fresh flower arrangements are on all the tables, and we've ordered special displays for the top table. Can you phone the florists and check arrangements there?

ASSISTANT: Sure.

CO-ORDINATOR: On Saturday there isn't much change to the original. We still don't know the titles of the workshops – they'll have to tell us before we do the final print. The afternoon tour is all arranged. You've booked the guide, haven't you?

ASSISTANT: Yes, we just need to confirm exact numbers – but we won't really know that until the day.

CO-ORDINATOR: Well, there's not much we can do about that. Just leave it – they won't mind.

ASSISTANT: I was thinking: why don't we include a stop for afternoon tea on the tour? There's a very nice place in the Trossachs I know.

CO-ORDINATOR: That's not a bad idea. Look into it, will you? The dinner on Saturday is more or less OK, I think, but they want to start a little later, at eight o'clock.

ASSISTANT: OK. We've still got to get the special table menus back from the printers.

CO-ORDINATOR: Oh yes, I'm glad you remembered that. Also they want the dinner to be followed by dancing. Apparently the hotel can provide a very good band.

ASSISTANT: Is that an extra cost?

CO-ORDINATOR: Yes, it wasn't on the original costing, so make sure it goes on the invoice. I think that's it. Oh, except that Basil Carter isn't able to come and do the closing session. It's going to be his partner – Peter Jenkins, I think he's called. It's the same subject, though. All the other speakers have confirmed, haven't they?

ASSISTANT: Yes, and I've confirmed their rooming arrangements.

CO-ORDINATOR: Oh, yes, and don't forget to ensure there are plenty of taxis available from around two o'clock on the Sunday. Have a word with the head doorman.

ASSISTANT: OK.

Unit 11

2 Listening

INTERVIEWER: George, you've been working for one of Europe's largest tour operators for the past twenty years. Can you tell us what familiarization trips are?

GEORGE: Well, the familiarization trip or 'fam trip', as it is commonly known, means different things to different people. Basically, for us, it is an opportunity for the people who sell our holidays to get to know our hotels and resorts better. We, as a tour operator, get together with an airline, the relevant national tourist office, and one or more of our hotels to construct a trip for the employees of the travel agencies that we're dealing with. They will be staying in our hotels, which, we hope, they will then recommend to their customers. Now, in the past, this was really often seen as a chance for, basically, a cheap holiday. You stayed in a nice hotel, met a few people and had a good time. Not much work was done. It was considered a kind of freebie.

INTERVIEWER: But not any more?

GEORGE: Well, I think those days have long gone. In the current economic climate, everyone is looking for value for money. No one's got money to throw around. Organizations invest in fam trips in the hope of securing extra business. In the past, we simply saw familiarization trips as a kind of reward. These days, that's still important but we emphasize much more the learning or the 'educational' side. Of course, we want people to have fun, but we need to see a return for our money. We want to make sure they go away with a good knowledge of our resorts and hotels. Any agency employee who comes on one of our fam trips is given a questionnaire to fill in while they are staying in the hotel, and we always ask for a report to be written afterwards. In that sense they're educational.

INTERVIEWER: You said earlier that fam trips were an opportunity for people to meet each other, but isn't it true that it's always the same kind of company that gets invited on fam trips – by that I mean the big ones?

GEORGE: Well, yes and no. Clearly we cannot send every employee in every agency on a familiarization trip. The important thing is to reward customer loyalty. So then we'll ask a good agency to send along a member of staff who has probably never stayed in one of our hotels before to come and see exactly what our hotels have to offer. Naturally, popular agencies sell more of our holidays, so more of their employees will go on our fam trips.

INTERVIEWER: Right. So it's a question of how popular a travel agency is?

GEORGE: Yes, but then there are the new-product educational trips. They may be quite different. Maybe our new hotels will appeal to travel agents that we don't do much, or even any, business with. When we have new hotels we wish to promote, we have to calculate which agencies to approach Then we do deals with smaller agencies. All

businesses need to evolve, so we can't just use the same hotels or the same travel agencies year after year.

INTERVIEWER: So who pays for fam trips?

GEORGE: Well, as I said: tour operators, transportation companies, such as airlines, but also coach companies and ferry operators and the hotels themselves. We actually charge the agencies something for sending people along. That way agencies themselves become more concerned about getting value for money. We don't charge much, mind, or we wouldn't get anyone who was interested.

INTERVIEWER: Right. Will you be sending people out soon?

GEORGE: Not right now, but we'll be sending people out in May, nearer the high season. Then by June we'll have arranged some more trips for the end of the summer, when we're not so busy. We also try to make sure that we send people who are in more or less the same positions in their firms. We don't usually have junior staff and senior management together, for example. They might feel a bit uncomfortable.

INTERVIEWER: Right. Well, thanks very much.

7 Listening

INTERVIEWER: Diane, can you tell me about your work and how you go about selecting a hotel for your clients?

DIANE: Well, I work exclusively with incentive tours. More precisely, I work as a Ground Handling Agent for incentive tours from the US. As I'm based here in London, I often don't know the clients intimately. So I rely on my incentive agent in the US to inform me of exactly what sort of group they are and what sort of things they like doing, etc. Then I'll make preliminary inspections of various hotels, as part of the job of a ground handler is selecting a hotel. The next thing is to make recommendations to my client on the basis of these inspections. Nine times out of ten, my clients will also want to inspect the hotels themselves, so one or two of my clients will come over on an inspection visit and they'll make the final choice themselves.

INTERVIEWER: Really?

DIANE: Yes, and we'll see as many hotels in one day as we can. A few days ago, I took some clients to visit seven hotels in one day, which is quite normal, but a few weeks ago, we inspected fourteen hotels all in one day.

INTERVIEWER: Goodness! What, in general, are they looking for?

DIANE: Obviously, details depend on the group in question. The incentive groups I deal with will generally spend a lot of time socializing. Consequently, the communal areas such as the bar must be large, attractive, and atmospheric. The reception area will be the first thing they see, so the company will want it to be impressive. Because there's lots of socializing, not just within the group but also with clients based in Europe, there must be sufficient rooms for private functions. And of course they've got to be big enough. Generally, that means we deal with luxury hotels. We don't always, because a de luxe hotel won't necessarily suit the requirements of the particular group we're dealing with. But, by and large, the more stars a hotel has, the bigger and better the facilities.

INTERVIEWER: So how do you keep up to date with new facilities, special offers, or even new hotels?

DIANE: I'm on the mailing list of all the main hotels in the London area so I'm kept updated by mailshot, and I know the people in the sales divisions of most of the hotels we deal with. If they have a special offer coming up, they'll telephone and let me know. To keep myself informed, there's the TTG – that's the Travel Trade Gazette – which is vital reading for anyone in my line of work. If there's any new hotel development, or even new hotels being built, then it will be included in there. I also make a point of going to trade fairs, such as the one in Earls Court in November called the WTM. People from all over the world attend, and I make appointments to meet people in the hotel business.

INTERVIEWER: Have you ever recommended a hotel you haven't inspected?

DIANE: Never. For example, yesterday I went into London just to see one room in a large city-centre hotel. I was offered forty-four of a particular type of room for a client. This hotel has fourteen different types and I wasn't sure it was the right type. Just to be sure, I went to check, and I'm glad I did. It wasn't! You see, every time I recommend a room, my reputation is on the line. I can't afford to make mistakes.

Unit 12

1 Listening

PETER: OK, so what time did they say they would be here, Donald?

DONALD: Well, they should be here at any moment.

PETER: Fine. Shall I complete the group check-in list when they get here?

DONALD: That's a good idea, and I'll give you some help if you need it. Good, here they are. Good morning! Welcome to the Fir Tree Hotel.

MRS ENDO: Good morning. My name is Megumi Endo. I'm the Tour Leader of the Endo Tour Group. Very nice to meet you.

DONALD: Good morning, Mrs Endo. I trust you had a pleasant flight. My name is Donald Carter, and I'm the Front Office Manager. I'll be checking you in. And this is Peter Makeland, my assistant. I have here your registration cards. Could you please ask your group to fill in both their names and passport numbers on the cards?

MRS ENDO: Yes, of course, thank you. Now we might have a small problem. Three of our group are friends, and they'd be happier if they shared a room. If they had told me earlier, I would have faxed you. I hope that's not inconvenient.

DONALD: No, not at all. So that's three fewer singles and one more triple, so that's two fewer rooms in total. That won't be a problem. Do you have the names? . . . Good, thank you. I'll get an updated rooming list printed, give it to the Head Porter and then he'll be able to make sure all the luggage is taken to the right rooms. They all have their names on their luggage?

MRS ENDO: Yes.

DONALD: Good, that's fine. The Head Porter will take care of that.

MRS ENDO: Can I give you my passport list?

DONALD: Thank you.

MRS ENDO: But I'm afraid I've left my voucher in my luggage. Can I give it to you later?

DONALD: Yes, of course. That won't be a problem. Now, I'm afraid *we* have a small problem. Because you are such a large group and it is so early in the morning, not all the rooms are quite ready. So, I've just bleeped the Food and Beverage Manager and she will be coming down in a minute to see to your food and drinks requirements while you are here.

MRS ENDO: Fine, thank you.

DONALD: Well, in fact, here she is. Mrs Endo, may I introduce you to Patricia Clarke, our Food and Beverage Manager. [hello, hello.] Patricia will take you through to the breakfast lounge and discuss your meal requirements. Thank you, Patricia.

MRS ENDO: Fine. Thank you.

DONALD: OK, Peter. Have you got everything?

PETER: Not quite. What room did we allocate the tour leader?

DONALD: Three-oh-four. And that's Megumi with an 'i' at the end.

PETER: OK, and the rooms. That's three fewer singles and one more triple. Twenty-four, ten, three and thirty-seven?

DONALD: That's right, so the total is two fewer. Under 'additional remarks', make a note to tell Reception of the changes. Put something like 'tell Reception two fewer rooms required', then you can tick it off when we've done that. You've made a note about the voucher, haven't you? [yes.] Good.

PETER: Fine, and Patricia Clarke – is that Clarke with an 'e' at the end?

DONALD: Yes, that's right. If you give me the sheet, I'll just check it and sign it.

PETER: There you are.

DONALD: OK . . . Fine. Now, let's go and join them in the breakfast lounge.

6 Listening

INTERVIEWER: I'd like to start by asking, have members of the BITOA noticed any changes over the last few years in what tourists are looking for?

RICHARD TOBIAS: Well, yes, there's been one very discernible change in recent years. By that I mean, and I'm only talking about in-bound tourists here, there's been a general trading-down of accommodation at the middle to top end of the market. Nowadays, a lot of tourists who were staying in four-star hotels a few years ago will now be looking at three-star.

INTERVIEWER: Oh, why's that?

RICHARD TOBIAS: There's one very good reason for it and that's the general world recession. So visitors are seeking value for money. Obviously, one very good way of cutting costs is to look at your major items of expenditure, such as your accommodation. The question is, of course, 'Will it continue?' Well, who knows. The paradox is that over the last few years, there have been more five-star hotels built than ever before. So perhaps they have suffered most.

INTERVIEWER: So what have hotels done about that?

RICHARD TOBIAS: They've had to improve their cost effectiveness, on the one hand, but at the same time, they have found perhaps that greater efficiency is not enough, and they've had to discount the price of their rooms as well. Most hotels in the present climate are willing to negotiate on price much more than they were in the past.

INTERVIEWER: Right, thanks. Inclusive tours, of course, provide an important source of income for hotels. Is there any truth in the accusation that there has been a lowering in standards of service because tour operators have recently been driving such a hard bargain?

RICHARD TOBIAS: None whatsoever. Tour operators, of course, want to operate to comfortable profit margins, but there's no evidence that this leads to a lowering of standards in hotels – quite the opposite. As a matter of fact, we receive a very low percentage of complaints, in terms of hotels. That's because, generally speaking, we, the British, provide a good service and very good value.

INTERVIEWER: Are tourists more, or less satisfied with the accommodation they are provided with?

RICHARD TOBIAS: It has always been the case that visitors of some nationalities have slightly different expectations from what hotels in this country are able to provide. Americans, for example, are used to very large hotel rooms by British standards. However, most of them know what to expect when they come here. The problem with people from some countries is that they don't complain until they get home! But, no, it's not an increasing tendency. We find the vast majority of our visitors are more than satisfied with the accommodation they receive.

INTERVIEWER: Have they noticed any other changes?

RICHARD TOBIAS: There is a growing awareness of the whole range of opportunities on offer in a country like Britain. People these days know there is more to Britain than the Tower of London. There is a larger base of second-time visitors who are already familiar with the traditional tourist locations and they're looking for something different.

INTERVIEWER: But haven't second-time visitors got a tendency to want to organize their own itineraries?

RICHARD TOBIAS: Oh, yes. But that's partly why tour operators these days offer so much more. Not so many years ago, the standard itinerary offered not much more than a visit to the major sights of London, a pub lunch, some more sightseeing, a restaurant followed by the theatre. Of course, there were always some special-interest groups but they were in the minority. These days there is much greater interest in tours such as the British Heritage Tours, which might involve guests visiting buildings of historic interest in more remote parts of the country. There are also British Industrial Heritage Tours. We even have special British Gourmet Tours where guests get to savour real traditional English food!

INTERVIEWER: Well, that's certainly different. How has this affected hotels?

RICHARD TOBIAS: Naturally, some hotels in less visited areas have benefited. Also, York, for example, which has always attracted a certain amount of tourism through the Minster, now finds its hotels are getting busier because of the growth of interest in British Heritage Tours.

INTERVIEWER: How does the future look?

RICHARD TOBIAS: It's looking good. The high season is just about over, but we are already looking forward to the next.

Wordlist

A

48-hour release p. 71
abundant p. 105
access to p. 165
accessible p. 13
accompanying p. 140
additional extras p. 164
adjoining p. 15
adjusting p. 27
admission p. 144
adventurous p. 89
aiding p. 46
air-conditioned p. 15
allocate a room p. 155
allocation (Allocation Holder) p. 71
alternative p. 128
amenities p. 15
annexe p. 152
annoyed p. 82
answerable to p. 153
aperitif p. 57
apology p. 81
appalling p. 161
apprentice p. 40
archaeological site p. 89
arguing p. 86
assemble p. 125
assist p. 135
at your disposal p. 114
at your fingertips p. 103
attentiveness p. 141
attic p. 29
attractions p. 98
Autocue p. 110
availability chart p. 71

B

baked p. 55
baize p. 114
bargaining p. 34
bill p. 67
bleep p. 133
boasts p. 130
bonus p. 151
brochure p. 18
budget p. 29
buffet service p. 15
bungalows p. 15
business centre p. 151

C

cabin p. 12
calculate p. 158
calm or calm down p. 78
cancellation fee or charge p. 93
candidate p. 38
canvass p. 141
capacity p. 112
carpenter p. 40
carved p. 55
cash p. 68
catering (for) p. 128
catering for p. 128
celebrated p. 13
chain p. 18
chambermaids p. 31
check out p. 68
check something through p. 158
cheque p. 68
child-proof p. 94
clientele p. 34
cloakroom p. 103
coated in p. 55
collision damage waiver (CDW) p. 94
comes to p. 67
comes under the remit of p. 154
command of p. 37
commentary p. 93
commission p. 66
communal rooms p. 29
complain p. 85
complaint *n* p. 78
complimentary p. 160
conducive to p. 103
conference rooms p. 22
conferences p. 20
confirmation p. 48
conservatory p. 126
conveniences p. 13
converted into p. 23
cope with p. 78
corporate client p. 46
cost effectiveness p. 171
counterparts p. 107
courteous p. 36
courtesy bus p. 26
credit card p. 68
crisp p. 55
cross-cultural training p. 105
crucial p. 101

cruise p. 89
crunchy p. 55
crust p. 55
currency p. 73
current p. 59
custom-made p. 121

D

day-to-day p. 32
de luxe p. 151
dealings with sb p. 154
delegates p. 37
deposit p. 69
deposited p. 59
designate p. 105
designated areas p. 151
dessert p. 56
disabled p. 20
disastrous p. 86
discernible p. 170
discount p. 71
discreet p. 114
disgusting p. 81
dispatch of luggage p. 154
distinguish between p. 164
double-checked p. 101
dressing-gown p. 105
dressing-table p. 59
driving a hard bargain p. 171
drop-off p. 93
duties p. 34
dust p. 80
duty manager p. 164

E

elaborate p. 12
empty p. 80
en suite p. 153
enhance p. 40
entails p. 39
entertainment p. 98
entrance charge p. 93
entrance fees p. 90
equipment p. 59
equipped with p. 94
escorting p. 138
evolve p. 168
exceptionally p. 24
exchange rate p. 73
exclusively for p. 114
excursion p. 90
exhibition p. 93

expand p. 13
expiry date p. 69
extension p. 23
external to p. 36

F

facilities p. 10
facility p. 59
fam(iliarization) trip p. 122
farewell p. 105
fee p. 12
filthy p. 81
fire escape p. 29
fitness centre p. 22
flexibility p. 46
flip-chart p. 103
flooding p. 105
folder p. 59
folk dancing p. 15
for inclusion p. 98
fort p. 144
Free Sale Agents p. 71
freebie p. 167
full-length mirrors p. 153
furnishings p. 24

G

garlic p. 54
garnish p. 54
goods p. 119
gourmet p. 171
group traffic p. 121
guaranteed p. 90
guidance p. 121

H

have a preference for p. 156
heavy workload p. 34
herbs p. 55
heritage p. 138
high season p. 15
hire p. 89
hoists p. 26
homely p. 153
honeymoon p. 17
honeymooners p. 105
horticulture p. 40
hospitality board p. 135
hospitality p. 15

174

hosting p. 140
hoteliers p. 34

ignored p. 78
imprint p. 69
in advance p. 13
in the event of sth p. 128
in-bound p. 170
in-house training p. 40
incentive tours p. 168
included p. 93
inclusive of p. 94
incoming p. 121
inspects p. 127
install p. 29
integration p. 46
interconnecting with p. 103
itinerary p. 125

juicy p. 55

kept updated p. 169
kettle p. 105
key card p. 159
king-size p. 27
know intimately p. 168

lapels p. 78
laundry p. 59
laundry/valet service p. 20
lay on p. 115
leaflet p. 130
lectern p. 110
lecture p. 110
leisure p. 135
liaise p. 37
linguists p. 105
liqueur p. 54
live music p. 15
loaded with sth p. 103
lobby p. 87
local authorities p. 140

lodge p. 13
log-book p. 36
luxurious p. 12

mailing list p. 169
mailshot p. 169
maintenance staff p. 40
major items of expenditure p. 170
make excuses p. 85
manual p. 42
market segments p. 46
mass-market tour operator p. 141
matching p. 46
mediator p. 140
meet sb's requirements p. 47
mileage p. 94
modules p. 46

nappy-changing facilities p. 26
National Trust p. 125
negotiates p. 71

occupancy rates p. 152
off my own bat p. 165
on hand p. 114
on request p. 114
on the line p. 169
onward travel p. 154
outdoor p. 130
outside contractors p. 40
overall vision p. 153
overbooking p. 128
overcooked p. 161

package p. 136
panoramic p. 153
pastry p. 54
pax p. 90
paying off p. 152
performing groups p. 121
permits p. 13
personal touch p. 34

personnel p. 31
petrol p. 53
pick-up p. 93
plasters p. 53
platters p. 59
play p. 93
play-room p. 26
plumber p. 40
potential p. 46
precautions p. 128
preliminary p. 168
press conference p. 110
prior to p. 47
private function rooms p. 136
process guests p. 46
product launch p. 110
profit margins p. 171
profitable p. 153
promote p. 168
promotional p. 129
prompt p. 105
provision for sth p. 47
public address (PA) system p. 110

Q

queries p. 154
questionnaire p. 123

R

ramps p. 26
range from ... to p. 13
receipt p. 68
recession p. 170
reclining p. 93
recommendation p. 29
recreation p. 20
rectify p. 141
reducing p. 46
refer to sb p. 48
refit p. 29
remedy p. 142
remote control p. 24
repair p. 80
replaster p. 80
require p. 50
requirement p. 49
reservationist p. 46
resort p. 15
resort representative p. 140
restricted to p. 107
retained p. 59
retrieve p. 48

revenues p. 46
roasted p. 54
room rack p. 47
room rate p. 65
room service p. 24
rooming list p. 139
ruins p. 162
rural p. 83
rustic p. 12

S

sachets p. 105
safety rail p. 29
sales outlet p. 69
sales/field force p. 107
sanitary facilities p. 13
savour p. 171
screen p. 103
seasonal p. 55
seasoned p. 54
second to none p. 114
self-contained p. 15
seminar p. 110
service charge p. 68
session p. 78
sessions p. 109
settling your account p. 50
sightseeing p. 98
skills p. 38
slices p. 54
slide projector p. 111
smart p. 40
snails p. 54
soaking p. 105
socializing p. 169
solarium p. 20
spacious p. 16
sparsely furnished p. 13
spectacular p. 115
speech p. 110
spelling out p. 128
spicy p. 54
split into p. 13
stables p. 12
stadium p. 93
staff p. 34
stair-lift p. 29
starter p. 56
stationery p. 103
statistical adj p. 42
statistics p. 46
status p. 164
sturdy p. 12
subtle p. 24
suite p. 12

superstition p. 105
supervise p. 61
surrounding p. 92
survey p. 141
sweep p. 80
switchboard p. 59
sympathized p. 78

T

tailoring sth to sb's needs p. 46
take sb's contact details p. 48
take-over p. 152
tap p. 53
tariff p. 59
tasteless p. 161
tasty p. 55
teletext p. 103
the vast majority of p. 107
theatre p. 93
third party, fire and theft p. 94
threatened to p. 161
throughout p. 15
tile p. 80
tip p. 32
tip-top condition p. 40
top of the range p. 164
tour operators p. 167
tourist board p. 124
trading-down p. 170
trading-up p. 138
trail p. 12
trainees p. 78
transaction p. 46
transfers p. 135
travel co-ordinator p. 135
traveller's cheque p. 68
treble-checked p. 101
trouser-press p. 24
turnover of stock p. 34

U

unacceptable p. 82
unaccompanied p. 105
unwind p. 15
up-to-date p. 127
up-to-the-minute p. 46
use his discretion p. 153
utilizes p. 46

V

vacancy p. 140
vacate p. 58
vacation p. 163
vacuum p. 80
valuable p. 59
variety show p. 136
vegetarians p. 57
venue p. 101
VHS p. 103
video recorder p. 110
vital p. 169
voucher p. 69

W

weed p. 80
were obliged to p. 107
willing to do sth p. 171
within (easy) reach p. 151
work record p. 39
work shifts p. 33
workaholic p. 34
workshop p. 110